A Soul Framed in Christ

A Soul Framed in Christ

—— *Stephen Charnock on the Renewal of God's Image* ——

Frank L. Bartoe IV

FOREWORD BY
Joel R. Beeke

WIPF & STOCK · Eugene, Oregon

A SOUL FRAMED IN CHRIST
Stephen Charnock on the Renewal of God's Image

Copyright © 2021 Frank L. Bartoe IV. All rights reserved. Except for brief quotations in critical publications or reviews, no part of this book may be reproduced in any manner without prior written permission from the publisher. Write: Permissions, Wipf and Stock Publishers, 199 W. 8th Ave., Suite 3, Eugene, OR 97401.

Wipf & Stock
An Imprint of Wipf and Stock Publishers
199 W. 8th Ave., Suite 3
Eugene, OR 97401

www.wipfandstock.com

PAPERBACK ISBN: 978-1-5326-6303-1
HARDCOVER ISBN: 978-1-5326-6304-8
EBOOK ISBN: 978-1-5326-6305-5

10/28/21

To Bridgette my loving wife and faithful helpmate, who has continuously loved with a Christ-like love and my children Rhachel and Langley, who have both been a tremendous source of encouragement.

Contents

Foreword by Joel R. Beeke | ix
Acknowledgements | xi

I. Introduction | 1

II. The Structure of Conforming Reality—God's Holiness | 12
    a. Principle of Holiness   12
        i. Nature of Conformity   17
        ii. Reflection of Conformity   23
    b. Conclusion   26

III. Fraying the Strands of Conformity | 29
    a. Principle of Contrariety   29
        i. Nature of Contrariety   33
        ii. Effects of Contrariety   36
        iii. Anatomy of Contrariety   42

IV. Re-tethering the Strands of Conformity | 49
    a. The Necessity of Continuity in Conformity   52
    b. Creational Conformity—Regeneration   58
        i. The Substantive Reality of Grace   60
        ii. The Substantial Being of Grace   63
    c. Covenantal Substratum of Conformity   66

V. The Epistemological Strands of Conformity | 75
   a. Capacitating Nature of Conformity   80
      i. Speculative Strand   84
      ii. Practical Strand   87
      iii. Nexus of Speculative and Practical Strands   91
      iv. Experiential Strand   96
      v. Interest Strand   103

VI. The Pneumatological Aspect of Conformity | 106
   a. The Whole Trinity in the Soul's Conformity   108
   b. The Centrality of the Spirit in Conformity   110
   c. The Hemming of Conformity in the Soul   114

VII. Conclusion | 116

VIII. Application | 128

   Bibliography | 131

Foreword

THE CLASSIC REFORMED RESOURCE on the doctrine of God is *The Existence and Attributes of God* by Stephen Charnock (1628–1680). However, Charnock, who served as a chaplain to Henry Cromwell in Ireland and then as co-pastor with Thomas Watson in London, also published extensive studies on other theological subjects ranging from the evils of unbelief to the saving power of Christ's death, exaltation, and intercession. This book consists of a study of Charnock's doctrine concerning the renewal of God's image in man through Christ. It especially draws from the neglected but precious discourses on regeneration found in volume 3 of Charnock's *Works*. May it prove to be an impetus for further research on Charnock's broader theology.

Frank Bartoe originally wrote this study as his thesis for the Master of Theology program at Puritan Reformed Theological Seminary. It was a pleasure for me to oversee his labor on this project, and it is a pleasure to see his hard work come to print. Through the process of his research and writing, Frank exhibited a humble and teachable spirit that displays the likeness of Christ, who amazingly made himself the humblest of men though he is God the Son incarnate.

Charnock said, "No greater glory can be, than to be a conspicuous and visible image of the invisible, and holy, and blessed God." Surely a great part of our communion with God in Christ consists in bearing his image and making known the beauty of his holiness by our attitude, words, and actions. May God use this study to promote both a greater understanding of God's renewed image and a greater participation in it through our Lord Jesus Christ.

—Joel R. Beeke, Puritan Reformed Theological Seminary

Acknowledgements

I WOULD LIKE TO take this opportunity to acknowledge those who have been instrumental in assisting me in developing the ideas presented in this small volume. I am immensely indebted to my wife, Bridgette, who has provided incalculable aid through her love for me and the extension of comfort and encouragement to me at times in which I doubted my ability to finish. She has been my greatest cheerleader, exhorting me to continue this project through completion. My two children, Rhachel and Langley, for their loving support and encouragement through their words and continual prayers throughout my studies. Thank you, Bridgette, Rhachel, and Langley.

Gratitude should be extended to my parents, Tina and Frank, for all the ways you have expressed your incredible aid and your loving support that helped my family and me throughout this prolonged period of instruction.

I am deeply indebted to my dear friend, Gene Osborne, who pressed me in the development of my thought, both theologically and philosophically, throughout the various stages of my studies. God has used you to shape and mold me into the person I am today, and I am thankful for your persistent pressing of the various aspects of my system of thought.

I owe special thanks to Dr. Joel Beeke, who exposed me to a realm of Christianity that has profoundly impacted the substance of my theological understanding—experiential theology. This experiential knowledge has forever re-wired my theological and philosophical understanding of the knowledge of God.

ACKNOWLEDGEMENTS

    Finally, and most importantly, I would like to acknowledge the vast depths of God's grace for orchestrating the events to bring this small book to a successful conclusion and the Lord Jesus Christ where the beauty of God's holiness shines so radiantly, especially to a soul that has been stitched together by the needle of grace and the thread of holiness that the Spirit weaves throughout the totality of the soul's complexion.

—Frank L. Bartoe IV

1

Introduction

"Grace hath a soul-raising excellency," wrote Thomas Watson, "it is a divine sparkle that ascends; when the heart is divinely touched with the load-stone of the Spirit, it is drawn up to God . . . grace gives us conformity to Christ."[1] It is from this Watson concludes that a "gracious soul is the image of God curiously drawn with the pencil of the Holy Ghost; an heart beautified with grace [and] grace is the purest complexion of the soul, for it makes it like God."[2] The truth of this beauty of grace that manifests itself in the grace of a soul's complexion was no more accurate of anyone than in Stephen Charnock (1628–1680).[3]

---

1. Watson, "Discourses upon Christ's Sermon on the Mount," in *Select Works*, 2:463.
2. Watson, "Discourses upon Christ's Sermon on the Mount," in *Select Works*, 2:462.
3. Charnock, a Puritan divine, was educated at Emmanuel College, Cambridge, where he received his B.A. (1646) and M.A. (1649). There was a sizable degree of influence on Charnock's thinking from Moise Amyraut, Jean Daille, Francisco Suarez, and the Cambridge Platonists (Culverwell and Cudworth). See Siekawitch, *Balancing Head and Heart in Seventeenth-Century Puritanism, Stephen Charnock's Doctrine of the Knowledge of God*, 50. "If the number of citations are any indication it would appear that the School of Saumur in France made the largest impression on Charnock next to puritanism. In his *Works*, he cited Moise Amyraut 130 times and Jean Daille 79 times. The next largest number of citations of anyone not affiliated with the School of Saumur was the Roman Catholic Francisco Suarez with 44." Also, Charnock was well versed in the works of Augustine, Aquinas, and Calvin. There are some striking similarities between Aquinas and Charnock, especially in Charnock's work *The Existence and Attributes of God*. For a development of this connection, see the work by Dolezal, *God without Parts: Divine Simplicity and the Metaphysics of God's Absoluteness*. Some have identified Charnock as the "zenith of Puritan or English Reformed scholastic divinity" or as "a kind of humanist-scholastic

In his funeral sermon for Charnock, Mr. John Johnson, an early friend, and fellow-collegiate at Cambridge, echoes the truth of grace found in a soul when describing Charnock. He paints an image of a man whose heart was divinely touched and drawn up to God. Mr. Johnson, with striking imagery, wanted it to be known that conforming grace was the defining characteristic of the man he knew personally. "He was," says Mr. Johnson, "the rational house of God, Christ's spiritual building, the temple of the Holy Ghost, framed and made up of orthodox doctrines and good works."[4] Although it would seem that such a characterization of a person would be enough to capture the essence of a man and his life, Johnson discloses something more fundamental than the "pencil of the Holy Ghost" and its drafting on Charnock's soul. According to Johnson, Charnock was

> [a] person transformed into the very image of God himself. Always serving the only true and living God, as becomes of such a God. All the work wherein he employed and exercised himself with diligence, skill, and constancy, was love to God and souls. His life, he examined and squared, until it was exactly according to the rule of God's word.[5]

It would seem, to some extent, that Mr. Johnson was either extracting concepts from Charnock's writings or was making a perceptive observation about his life. Either way, it speaks to the continuity associated with Charnock's life and writings.

The reality of this observation becomes readily apparent if one was to read Charnock's writings with Mr. Johnson's assessment that he was a

---

who stood on the middle ground between linguistics and metaphysics." Charnock wrote extensively on many different topics; however, he is best known for his two-volume work *The Existence and Attributes of God*, and this is only two of five volumes of his published works. Perhaps, the extensive nature of his works is one of the reasons for the scant secondary work on Charnock. See Beeke and Jones. *A Puritan Theology: Doctrine for Life*, 59. In addition to his solid biblical exposition of Scripture, we see Charnock's training in scholastic theology and philosophy express itself in his works on God's providence and attributes, as well as in his writings on regeneration and knowledge of God. See Beeke and Pederson, *Meet the Puritans*, 145. This last work is described as "a bit tedious, yet is eminently scriptural and experiential." Some do take issue with Charnock and his work on the attributes of God. See Hoek, "God Nearby and God Far Away-Stephen Charnock on Divine Attributes," 7. See also Gunton, *Act & Being: Towards Theology of the Divine Attributes*.

4. Middleton, "Stephen Charnock, B.D.," *Biographia Evangelica*, 445.
5. Middleton, "Stephen Charnock," 445.

"person really transformed into the very image of God himself."[6] This "very image of God" is a more conscious thought than all other things noted about Charnock; as a matter of fact, it could be suggested that the other attributes pale in the shadow of this image of God in Charnock. Indeed, his life was nothing more than an outflowing from the reality contained in "a person really transformed into the very image of God himself."[7] The significance of this assessment by Mr. Johnson will be borne out in various areas of this paper, and its truth will be manifested. What is most striking about this assessment of Mr. Johnson is that what he saw in this man— Charnock—is what appears to be the critical focus of Charnock's studies. Johnson identified the reality that in Charnock, "the very image of God" was a regulating principle for his life and the beauty of grace functioning as a bonding agent for the totality of his theological thought.

There is a similar assessment of Charnock set forth by James M'Cosh, professor of logic and metaphysics at Queen's College in Belfast, where he seems to note the internal substance of that image of God which Charnock sought to understand. According to M'Cosh, Charnock's longing desire that he would, at some point, obtain "the perfection of grace and holiness."[8] This longing desire serves as a backdrop for Charnock, and it demonstrates itself in every sermon where he seeks to explore the depths of the attributes of God and his truth, mercy, grace, and goodness. Also, it manifests itself in Charnock's relentless pursuit to comprehend the glorious truths of the "perfection of grace and holiness" and its fashioning effect as the "purest complexion of the soul." Consequently, both Mr. Johnson's and M'Cosh's valuation of Charnock as a man of God coalesces around the same regulating principle, with one encapsulating it within the image of God and the other pointing to the substance of that image in the connective reality of grace and holiness. Nonetheless, they had ascertained a fundamental component of Charnock's theology that is found throughout his writings and pinpointed by his co-pastor,[9] Thomas Watson, that "grace gives us conformity to Christ," and the beauty of that conformity is reflected in the complexion of a soul that has been framed in Christ.

---

6. Middleton, "Stephen Charnock," 445.

7. Middleton, "Stephen Charnock," 445.

8. Charnock, The Complete Works of Stephen Charnock, in *Works,* 1: xxv.

9. Charnock, "Introduction to Charnock's Works," in *Works,* 1: xxiii. The last five years of Charnock's life (1675–1680) was spent as a "joint pastor to the Rev. Thomas Watson in Crosby Hall."

It is the sustaining reality of that beauty and conformity that we will find Charnock consistently employing, that he will ground in the reality of grace and holiness, which has effectively altered the substantive nature of the soul's structure. In addition, this grace and holiness will function as an interpretative grid for understanding the framing of the soul in Christ. For Charnock, grace expands the entirety of creation in some respect; however, the place to see the most glorious operations of redemptive grace is to look upon the nature of the soul to get a sight of Christ weaving those fibers of grace and holiness throughout the totality of the soul. In his works, he depicts the Puritan's perspective of God's grace and holiness as the "central force of heaven"[10] that permeates the whole realm of the soul's environment. That is, it is the backdrop, the foundation, the lineaments, and is a living constituent of spiritual reality that has been sent forth with a primary mission, from the Creator, to lay claim to that which was lost. It is within this context that Charnock's understanding of the purpose of redemptive grace, which, by its very design, is meant to reclaim God's most prized creation that was created to be a reflection of his glory: his holiness—the image of God. It is to this end that this study will attempt to explore Charnock's doctrine of redemptive grace in the renewal of God's image in the soul and its relation to God in covenant, his divine beauty, and man's chief end to redound the glory of God in the temporal, as well as the heavenly realm.

What will become evident as we explore Charnock's doctrine of the renewal of God's image in the soul is that implicit within Charnock's understanding of the image of God in the soul is the notion of conformity. This notion of conformity[11] is a fundamental theme that is laced throughout Charnock's *Discourses*, especially in light of the contrasting reality that he identifies as "a principle of contrariety." This principle of contrariety describes the reality that the deforming nature of sin has replaced the beauty of the soul. As a result, several questions surface: the nature of conformity,

---

10. Smith, *Select Discourses*, l. The is a real force and "Tis not," says Smith, "the Speculation of Heaven as a thing to come that satisfies the desires of religious souls, but the real possession of it even in this life."

11. It was a fundamental theme for Puritans, in general, because it was a reality that stood in opposition to the depraved nature of man. "Sin is," the Catechism states, "any want of conformity to the law of God, or transgression of it." See Westminster Assembly, *The Westminster Confession of Faith: Edinburgh Edition*, 391. The epicenter of this conformity is often identified with what seems to be one favorite passage of Scripture for the Puritans: "But we all, with unveiled face, beholding as in a mirror the glory of the Lord, are being transformed into the same image from glory to glory, just as from the Lord, the Spirit" (2 Cor 3:18).

the object of conformity, the standard of conformity, the congruity inherent within conformity, as well as the extent of conformity. For Charnock, these various aspects of conformity address an essential relationship that ushers the creature into the presence of his Creator, and this relationship defines the content of questions, such as: Is there a greater excellency than for a creature to be found in conformity to God? What more magnificent beauty could be obtained than a soul to be framed in grace and holiness? How can the creature be conformed to God with a nature that stands in conflict with his framing? How can any soul conform to God without that which essentially constitutes that conformity? Can there be a semblance to God without a semblance to his holiness? What is necessary for the soul to resemble God in its nature? What is the substance of that divine beauty when it is formed in the disposition of the soul? How does one account for conformity in a realm of contrariety? However, all those questions are but variant parts of the one predominant notion of conformity that thoroughly captivated Charnock's attention and which he expresses in the following question: "Can there be a greater excellency than to have a divine beauty, a formation of Christ, a proportion of all graces, suited to the imitable perfections of God?"[12]

The concept of the soul's highest excellence, its most excellent conformity, that is expressed in the previous question is not isolated to one particular discourse in Charnock's works. Instead, it appears in various discourses, for example, and although the wording is different, the substance of the question is maintained and expressed in the following: in *The Necessity of Regeneration*, he makes a statement that reflects the notion contained in the above question: "The perfection of everything," says Charnock, "consists in answering the end for which it was framed. That which was the first end of our framing, ought to be the end of our acting, viz. the

---

12. Charnock, "The Nature of Regeneration," in *Works*, 3:135 "No greater glory can be, than to be a conspicuous and visible image of the invisible, and holy, and blessed God." See Charnock, "A Discourse upon the Holiness of God," in *Works*, 2, 269. This correlates to Charnock's perspective that while we are here in this temporal realm, the heavenly reality has been established within the soul. "Heaven is not so much an outward as an inward life; the foundation of glory is laid in grace; a resemblance to God is our vital happiness, without which the vision of God would not be so much as a cloudy and shadowy happiness, but rather a torment than a felicity; unless we be of a like nature to God, we cannot have a pleasing fruition of him." 2, 270. Therefore, Charnock states that we "should manage our hearts so as if we had a view of God in his heavenly glory." See Charnock, "A Discourse upon Spiritual Worship," in *Works*, 1:311.

glory of God."¹³ In *A Discourse on the Nature of Regeneration*, Charnock asks: "Can it be anything else but the highest excellency, to live the life of God; to have the image of God wrought upon you, and your souls conformed to his holiness?"¹⁴ The same idea is conveyed in a question posed in his *Discourse Proving Weak Grace Victorious*, "And how can we imagine anything, wherein we can be more like to God, than in that which is the highest excellency and perfection of God?"¹⁵ Again, in *A Discourse of the Efficient of Regeneration*, "Is it not our highest excellency to be conformed to God in holiness, in as full a measure as our finite natures are capable?"¹⁶ In *A Discourse of the Knowledge of God*, once again, he distills an ultimate perspective of this guiding aspect of his thought, "The sight of the beauty of God is the end of the soul, and what is the end of a thing is the perfection of it."¹⁷ It is evident that Charnock is working from the outer edges of this

13. Charnock, "The Necessity of Regeneration," in *Works*, 3:37.

14. Charnock, "The Nature of Regeneration," in *Works*, 3:161.

15. Charnock, "Weak Grace Victorious," in *Works*, 5:229.

16. Charnock, "The Efficient of Regeneration," in *Works*, 3:303. We find here that Charnock is identifying the two realms of reality and the inherent limitations to this temporal realm and the capacities associated with the temporal realm. In *A Discourse upon the Holiness of God*, Charnock states that "No greater glory can be, than to be a conspicuous and visible image of the invisible, and holy, and blessed God." 2:269. He also notes, "Since that good is the object of a rational appetite, the purest, best, and most universal good, such as God is, ought to be most sought after. Since good only is the object of a rational appetite, all the motions of our souls should be carried to the first and best good; a real good is most desirable; the greatest excellency of the creatures cannot speak them so, since by the corruption of man they are 'subjected to vanity,' Rom. 8:20. God is the most excellent good, without any shadow; a real something, without that nothing which every creature hath in its nature, Isa. 40:17." 2:391. John Calvin expressed the same thought when he noted: "There is, no doubt, a far more rich and powerful manifestation of Divine grace in this second creation than in the first; but our highest perfection is uniformly represented in Scripture as consisting in our conformity and resemblance to God. Adam lost the image which he had originally received, and therefore it becomes necessary that it shall be restored to us by Christ." John Calvin and William Pringle, *Commentaries on the Epistles of Paul to the Galatians and Ephesians*, 296.

17. Charnock, "The Knowledge of God," in *Works*, 4:94. Throughout Charnock's "Discourses," we find the influence of Aristotle and Thomas Aquinas, especially with such statements referenced above. It is interesting to note that "excellence is a perfection," says Aristotle, "for when anything acquires its proper excellence we call it perfect, since it is then if ever that we have one as good as possible, while defect is a perishing of or departure from this condition" *Physics* 246a13–16. Also, Aristotle, "ETHICA EUDEMIA," in *The Works of Aristotle*, vol. 9. Aristotle states, "This is clear by induction; for in all cases we lay this down: e.g., a garment has an excellence, for it has a work and use, and the best state of the garment is its excellence. Similarly a vessel, house, or

ultimate reality of the soul's conformity to the highest excellence, and it directed his discourses that intentionally coalesced around his resolution to grasp the magnitude of the nature of that divine beauty in the soul (i.e., a reflection of God's imitable perfection).

Chapter 1: The Structure of Conforming Reality—God's Holiness

If the greatest or highest degree of excellence is found in this imitable perfection of God, this conformity to holiness, then what does this perfection or conformity look like in the soul? What does Charnock identify as the catalyst for the nature of that realization of this definitive perfection in the soul which establishes this divine beauty and frames the intrinsic nature of the soul that it is bent on redounding to the glory of those imitable perfections of God? Chapter 1 will explore the answers that Charnock offers up to such questions; more specifically, we will consider God's holiness and the conformity to that holiness that is attributed to a soul renewed in the image of God.

In light of Charnock's understanding of God's holiness and the soul's conformity to that holiness, we will consider the implications of that conformity as it pertains to the relation that the creature stands in the Creator-creature relationship because man is capable of standing in more than just the Creator-creature relationship with God. There is a Redeemer-redeemed relation, and the conformity of the soul to its object will directly bear upon man's relational standing before God.[18] That is, all men stand in relation to

---

anything else has [5] an excellence; therefore so also has the soul, for it has a work." See Flavel, "What is the life of glory but the vision of God, and the soul's assimilation to God by that vision?" in *Works*, 2:95.

18. To avoid any ambiguity or suggestion of forensic justification, the phrase "relational standing before God" is not meant to suggest that man is capable of justifying himself by his holiness. This "relational standing before God" speaks to the fact that the creature does stand in relation to God as his Creator. As for the redeemed soul, the new creature stands in a Redeemer-redeemed relation, and as a depraved, unredeemed soul, he stands in a Judgment-judged or condemned relation. This relational standing could be expressed in covenantal terms, such as one who is identified as a covenant-keeper or covenant-breaker. Since God is covenantal, man is either a covenant-keeper or a covenant-breaker; if the former, then in communion with God, and that communion is covenantal-communion. Puritans viewed covenantal-communion to be in covenant with God, which would mean a change in the covenant-state or covenant-relation with God. It was necessary for the Puritans to understand the great distance between God and man outside of covenantal-relations because of the covenant-defiant act of Adam that implicated the whole of humanity. So, the only logical conclusion would be heart

God as Creator; however, outside this relation, man either stands before God as a redeemed creature in Christ or condemned creature in his sin and depravity awaiting judgment. The former, being a redeemed soul that has been renewed in Christ, effectively changes the dynamics of man's standing before God to a Redeemer-redeemed relation. It is the vital principle of imputed holiness, which, for Charnock, intrinsically defines that relationship, and it functions as the basis for understanding the soul's conformity to God's imitable perfections.

Chapter 2: Fraying the Strands of Conformity

If God's holiness defines the conformity of the soul, then the entrance of sin into the world would be the corrosion of that conformity, that is, the reality that caused holiness in the soul to be undone. Chapter 2, will consider how Charnock explains this corrosion, which is nothing short of total depravity and the repercussions of the reality of this depravity. Although Charnock does not employ the phrase typically associated with the Reformed notion of man's fall into sin—total depravity—in his writings, he manages to convey and capture the comprehensiveness of it, as the seriousness of the reality of sin. This depravity that defines a soul outside of Christ is the existence of a principle that God did not implant in the soul. This, Charnock identifies in his writings, is a principle that stands in direct opposition to the principle of holiness—a principle of contrariety.[19] This defining principle of contrariety establishes a scriptural perspective for Charnock, and it manifests itself in the nature of the soul, which was initially created in the image of God.

Chapter 3: The Principle of Conformity

In chapter 3, Charnock's doctrine of renewing God's image is considered, more specifically, the reestablishing of the conformity of the soul to God's imitable perfections. It is clear from what has been outlined in the previous

---

conformity to God's covenant, which is a covenant-keeping-state that would be indicative of the covenantal-communion with their Creator God. However, for clarity's sake, it is essential to remember that man is always covenantally connected or grounded to the Creator and is incapable of breaking free from this reality, no matter how far down he entrenches himself in his covenant-defiant position.

19. Charnock, "Man's Enmity against God," in *Works*, 5:463.

chapters that the notion of conformity in the soul has been usurped by a foreign notion of deformity, a deformity of what was originally created in conformity to God's holiness. So, what is required for the reality of deformity to be replaced with conformity? The essential reality entailed in the transition from a state of deformity to that of conformity to God's holiness is what Charnock will squarely root in the redemptive work of Christ. This redemptive work speaks to a vital reality, and this vital reality directs us to consider the magnitude of grace in bringing the soul into this right-relationship with the Redeemer. More specifically, Charnock explains the extent of the "new-creating" grace where he perceives the glorious unfolding of God's providence "in the framing the soul to be a living monument of his glory."[20] That is, the framing of the soul is "the inward jewel wrapped up from the view of men; the spirit of the mind, which, being more excellent, requires more of skill for the new forming of it."[21] It is this internal structure that will bring into greater clarity the beauty of grace in establishing the framing of a soul in Christ, as we will see Charnock's understanding of the pervasive nature of God's grace working a new reality in the soul of man, as well as framing a new reality in the soul through Christ.

This is, in effect, a systematic investigation of the degree or the scope of God's grace in defining the various aspects that are intrinsic to a soul's nature framed in Christ. It is an exploration of the enormity of this "new-creating" grace that has dismantled the depraved nature of the soul and recreates the internal frame of the soul to reflect the glory, that imitable perfection, of its Redeemer. To grasp the immensity of this grace requires that we consider the natural makeup of the soul's disposition. That is, we need to address some underlying questions, such as: Is it the totality of the soul's environment that is shaped and formed by this "new-creating" grace? Does the nature of the right-relationship require that grace define the soul's atmosphere in its totality, or is it only sections of the soul's atmosphere? That is, can the nature of the soul truly take on the likeness of God's holiness outside the realm of this grace?

Chapter 4: The Epistemological Strands of Conformity

Chapter 4 will survey Charnock's epistemological theory as he perceives it to be structured in a soul that has been framed in Christ. It is a necessary and

20. Charnock, "The Efficient of Regeneration," in *Works*, 3:271.
21. Charnock, "The Efficient of Regeneration," in *Works*, 3:271.

logical transition to the knowledge of God from the consideration of God's grace in the previous section because, for Charnock, "it is not conceivable how grace can be without knowledge."[22] So this knowledge is intrinsically bound up with a soul that has been framed in Christ, especially in light of Charnock's perspective of grace and the substance of the soul. The inherent nature of this knowledge of God and Christ "is the chief ingredient which makes the composition of the inner man."[23]

This chapter will explore that chief ingredient that Charnock identifies as the "composition of the inner man." And we will see that, once again, the redemptive grace of Christ is the thread that weaves holiness throughout the construct of Charnock's theory of knowledge. So, it is with knowledge, as it was with man's existence, and relational standing with God (i.e., as Creator or Redeemer), that the nature of who God is must be the defining aspect of our reality in Christ, which is: our knowledge must be grounded in the "holiness of truth" (Eph 4:24). Therefore, we will explore the beauty of the implications of this holiness that redemptive grace has framed within the soul, more specifically, the conforming aspect of our knowledge to that holiness that was "the first deformity of man, and the cause of all the rest."[24] According to Charnock, "the knowledge of God is the first line the Spirit draws upon the soul, as from the first matter, all those beautiful graces that appears in every region of the soul are formed."[25] Therefore, we will reconnoiter the various layers of Charnock's epistemological structure (i.e., theory of knowledge), which he divides into the following categories: speculative, practical, experimental, and knowledge of interest.[26]

Chapter 5: The Pneumatological Aspect of Conformity

The final chapter is really a means to tie the totality of Charnock's thought together, or perhaps better stated, the chapter identifies the tethering point for Charnock's doctrine of the renewal of the image of God in the soul. The chapter will consider the totality of this divine beauty as it relates to

---

22. Charnock, "The Knowledge of God," in *Works*, 4:30.
23. Charnock, "The Knowledge of God," in *Works*, 4:30.
24. Charnock, "The Knowledge of God," in *Works*, 4:29.
25. Charnock, "The Knowledge of God," in *Works*, 4:29.
26. Siekawitch, *Balancing Head and Heart in Seventeenth Century Puritanism, Stephen Charnock's Doctrine of the Knowledge of God*. Siekawitch details the structure and the substance of Charnock's knowledge of God.

Charnock's trinitarian understanding of God's redemptive work within the framing of the soul in his image.

Will find that, for Charnock, the totality of this renewal of the image of God is ultimately established, defined, and brought into existence by the work of the Trinity. Furthermore, Charnock demonstrates the glorious unity of redemptive work in the Trinity—the centrality of the Trinity in taking a depraved soul and infusing life, not only life per se but hemming the principle of life—God's holiness—into a soul. The consideration of the Trinity, to some extent, brings us full circle in consideration of Charnock, and we will, once again, see the continuity in Charnock's theology, as well as his life. The perceptive Mr. Johnson observed in Charnock that his life was demarcated by a covenantal harmony, that is, "His life," says Mr. Johnson, "he examined and squared, until it was exact according to the rule of God's word."[27] Therefore, for Charnock, the fullness of that connective reality of God's grace and holiness is reflected in the fact that the redemptive work is a Trinitarian work in the soul.

---

27. Charnock, "Weak Grace Victorious," in *Works*, 5:229.

II

The Structure of Conforming Reality —God's Holiness

a. Principle of Holiness

THE PERIOD OF HIGH Orthodoxy (1640-1700) marked a point of significant doctrinal development and the codification of the doctrine of God, and there were several works produced that speaks to that development. For example, consider the following works that were produced during this period: Edward Leigh *(1602-1671)*, *A Treatise of Divinity Consisting of Three Bookes;* William Bridge (1606-1670), *Christ and the Covenant— Meditating on the Attributes of God* and *Grace for Grace—an Explanation of the Attributes of God;* Thomas Brooks (1608-1680), *The Attributes of God and Christ's Deity;* Francis Turretin (1623-1687), *Institutes of Eclentic Theology*[1]; William Bates (1625-1699), *The Harmony of the Divine Attributes in the Contrivance and Accomplishment of Man's Redemption;* George Swinnock (1627-1673), *A Treatise of the Incomparableness of God in His Being, Attributes, Works and Word;* Stephen Charnock (1628-1680), *Discourses upon the Existence and Attributes of God;* and Ezekiel Hopkins (1634-1690), *On Glorifying God in His Attributes.*

---

1. Turretin, *Institutes of Elenctic Theology*, 1:187-9. "Can the divine attributes be really distinguished from the divine essence?" and "Is the distinction of attributes into communicable and incommunicable a good one?" Turretin will address the following in his doctrine of God: simplicity, infinity, immensity, eternity, immutability, knowledge, will, justice, goodness, love, grace, mercy, power, dominion, and sovereignty of God.

Although all of these men made various contributions to the development of the doctrine of God, it seems that Charnock rises above the rest in terms of the magnitude of his contribution to the codification of the doctrine of God. Charnock's *Discourses upon the Existence and Attributes of God* is his *magnum opus;* it's where we see Charnock demonstrating his ability, according to Joel Beeke *et al.*, "to combine rigorous theological discourse on the doctrine of God with the typical Puritan emphasis on 'uses' of the doctrine of (relating doctrine and life)."[2] The Puritan emphasis found in this work is re-iterated and characterized by Richard Muller as "remaining firmly within the genre of devotional and homiletical theologies, the English writers Richard Baxter and Stephen Charnock wrote extensively on the divine attributes, with particular emphasis on the practical 'use' of their doctrine."[3]

In Charnock's various *Discourses*, we encounter the demarcation of the various attributes of the God of Scripture. Throughout these *Discourses*, Charnock is drawing from the deep well of Scripture to demonstrate the glorious unchanging reality of the transcendent God who is not "turned by the force of nature, nor changed by the accidents in the world, but sits

---

2. Beeke and Jones, *A Puritan Theology: Doctrine for Life*, 59. The development of the doctrine of God and its significance in a life of piety can be seen in the following works: Bates, *The Harmony of the Divine Attributes in the Contrivance and Accomplishment of Man's Redemption*; Hopkins, *On Glorifying God in His Attributes*, in *Works*, 2:590–708. Richard Muller speaks very highly of Charnock's *Discourses upon the Existence and Attributes of God*; see Muller, *Post-Reformation Reformed Dogmatics*, 3:132. Muller notes, "Also of considerable significance as both a contribution to the English Reformed theology of the seventeenth century and as a codification of doctrine evidencing the extensive resources and major opponents of the Reformed position is Charnock's *Discourses upon the Existence and Attributes of God* . . . Charnock's *Discourse* certainly stands as one of the more elaborate and detailed treatises on the subject written in the seventeenth century and, [it] partakes of the careful distinctions and definitions that belong to the scholastic theology of the era. It also evidences the exegetical and practical character of the Protestant theology of the era, with consistent references to the texts of Scripture on which its teaching is based and equally consistent attention to the churchly and pious 'use' of each doctrinal point. Charnock's work, remarkable for its grasp of the scholastic materials and for its ability to turn those materials to homiletical use, invariably turns toward christological and soteriological issues—perhaps most notably following the discussion of the attribute of spirituality with an entire homily on spiritual worship. Although, for the most part lacking in the polemical or the elenctical aspect of the Reformed theology of the day, Charnock's treatise echoes the fourfold concern for exegetical, doctrinal, polemical, and practical emphases exemplified in a continental work like Mastricht's great *Theoretico-practica theologia.*"

3. Muller, *Post-Reformation Reformed Dogmatics*, 3:116.

in the heavens, moving all things by his powerful arm, according to his infinite skill."[4] However, Charnock does not leave it as some disconnected abstract notion of a transcendent God bound to the heavens; instead, upon expounding on any given attribute of God, he then shows the tethering nature of that reality; the implications on the life of God's creatures. There is, in Charnock's thought, a continuity between the eternal reality and the temporal realm. For example, the necessity of the practical reality in the life of a believer is squarely grounded in the attributes of God. That is, all "the attributes of God," according to Charnock, "are the crutches of faith, the bladders upon which faith swims."[5] Moreover, these "glorious attributes bear a comfortable respect to believers."[6]

Although not to minimize any of the attributes of God, because all "the attributes of God," says Charnock, "have appeared in some beautiful glimmerings in the world;"[7] however, there is one particular attribute among the three great attributes of God[8] that was manifested in the height of God's creative act of his image, which did more than glimmer; it was a brilliant depiction of God's holiness. The particularity of the attribute of holiness is significant, especially when we consider "the creation of man, in a state of such perfection as to be endued with the image of God, was a greater work... because the attributes of God did more lively appear in him, and particularly his holiness."[9] We will return to the relation of the image of God and the attribute of holiness, more specifically, to consider the implication of a proper understanding of this relationship between the image and God's holiness, which bears out in a Reformed soteriological understanding.

---

4. Charnock, "A Discourse upon the Immutability of God," in *Works*, 1:419.
5. Charnock, "A Discourse of the Knowledge of God," in *Works*, 4:59.
6 Charnock, "A Discourse upon the Wisdom of God," in *Works*, 2:5.
7. Charnock, "A Discourse upon God's Knowledge," in *Works*, 1:512. See Charnock, *The Complete Works of Stephen Charnock*, 3:108. He points out that the applicability of God's attributes meets us at various points in our life. "As the attributes of God, though in the highest perfection, yet in their exercise in the world, sometimes one appears more triumphant than another, sometimes more of patience, sometimes mercy, sometimes justice, sometimes wisdom, one is more eminently apparent than another; so the divine nature hath seminally in this habit all grace, and an agreeableness to every duty enjoined, a principle to send forth the fruits of all when an object is offered, and the grace excited by the Spirit of God; yet sometimes one is more visible than another, according to the call it hath to stand forth and shew itself."
8. Charnock, "A Discourse of Divine Providence," in *Works*, 1:31. "You see upon the account of holiness, righteousness, goodness, the three great attributes of God."
9. Charnock, "A Discourse of the Efficient of Regeneration," in *Works*, 3:194.

Also, the attribute of holiness "hath an excellency above his other perfections"[10] moreover, none "is sounded out so loftily," Charnock states, "with such solemnity, and so frequently by angels that stand before his throne, as this."[11] He is emphatic in making his point about this particular attribute of God and is insistent about the significance of God's holiness.

Charnock asks first, "Where do you find any other attribute trebled in the praises of it, as this?"[12] Secondly, he asks, "Do we hear of any other divine attribute of God repeated three times over in the scriptures?"[13] Do we find it said of his wisdom? Of his mercy and grace? Of his infinity or immutability? Of his dominion or sovereignty? "Is there anywhere that we read in the scriptures," Charnock presses, "of the crying out Eternal, eternal, eternal; or Faithful, faithful, faithful, Lord God of hosts! Whatsoever other attribute is left out, this God would have to fill the mouths of angels and blessed spirits for ever in heaven."[14] All of these are answered in a negative because we do not find this to be the case when we survey the Scriptures for a threefold declaration of God. Instead, what we find in the Scriptures is the threefold pronouncement of God's holiness: "Holy, holy, holy, is the Lord of hosts;" declares Isaiah, "The whole earth is full of His glory!"[15] "Holy, holy, holy, Lord God Almighty, Who was and is and is to come!"[16] It is here that "His power of sovereignty as Lord of hosts," Charnock points out, "is but once mentioned, but with an eternal repetition of his holiness."[17]

The ultimacy of this attribute of God's holiness speaks to the fact that "God is," Swinnock says, "so incomparable in holiness that it is said, he only, or solely, is holy, Rev. 15:4, 'Who will not fear thee, O Lord, and glorify thy name? for thou only art holy.'"[18] No doubt, the words found in Rev 15:4 were echoing the glorious truth identified in the song of Moses offered up to the Lord in Exod 15:11, where he declares the Lord to be "glorious in holiness." In reference to that particular verse, Watson ascertains God's

---

10. Charnock, "A Discourse upon the Holiness of God," in *Works*, 2:191.
11. Charnock, "A Discourse upon the Holiness of God," in *Works*, 2:191.
12. Charnock, "A Discourse upon the Holiness of God," in *Works*, 2:191–92.
13 Charnock, "A Discourse upon the Holiness of God," in *Works*, 2:191–92.
14. Charnock, "A Discourse upon the Holiness of God," in *Works*, 2:192.
15. Isa 6:3 NKJV.
16. Rev 4:8 NKJV.
17. Charnock, "A Discourse upon the Holiness of God," in *Works*, 2:192.
18. Swinnock, *The Works of George Swinnock*, 4:404.

holiness as "the most sparkling jewel in the Godhead, Exod. 15:11"[19]; and as the "most sparkling jewel" it is of "an infinite stupendous height of excellency in God,"[20] says Jeremiah Burroughs.

What significance does God's holiness have in Charnock's developing his doctrine of the renewal of God's image in the soul? God's holiness is a fundamental substratum of reality that Charnock keeps at the center of his understanding of who God is and man's relation to him. Charnock demonstrates the significance of God's holiness in his summation of the Christian religion and the foundation of beauty. First, in the Christian religion, he reasons if "holiness be an eminent perfection of the divine nature," then the entirety of the "Christian religion is of a divine extraction. It discovers the holiness of God, and forms the creature to a conformity to him."[21] Secondly, inherent within the concept of beauty is the foundation of holiness; that is, the reality of "the beauties of holiness,"[22] which is noted in Ps 110:3 as the tethering point of what would be identified as the "excellency and beauty of a creature."[23] According to Charnock, the very "title of beauty is given to it [creature] in Ps. 110:3, beauties, in the plural number, as comprehending in it all other beauties whatsoever."[24] There is a substantive depth of reality

---

19. Watson, *The Select Works of the Rev. Thomas Watson*, 161. Watson explores this "sparkling jewel in the Godhead" in his sermon on "Of the Holiness of God." God is holy intrinsically: 1. He is holy in his nature; his very being is made up of holiness, as light is of the essence of the sun. —2. He is holy in his word; the word bears a stamp of his holiness upon it, as the wax bears an impression of the seal, Ps. 119:140., "Thy word is very pure;" it is compared to silver refined seven times, Ps. 12:6. Every line in the word breathes sanctity, it encourageth nothing but holiness. —3. God is holy in his operations; all God doeth is holy; he cannot act but like himself; he can no more do an unrighteous action, than the sun can darken, Ps. 145:17, "The Lord is holy in all his works." See Watson, "Of the Holiness of God," in *Works*, 59–60.

20. Burroughs, *The Saints Treasury*, 8.

21. Charnock, "A Discourse Upon the Holiness of God," in *Works*, 2:256. This notion of a "divine extraction" is a phrase that Charnock uses to identify the soul as "a soul of a heavenly extraction, formed by the breath of God, Gen. 2:7." Elsewhere in speaking of the nature derived from Adam and that derived from Christ notes, "they both imprint their image according to the quality of their extraction" (see the remaining quote). Also, interesting to note that God has instilled this notion within the mind of man, as evidenced by Aristotle, who notes: "Now the end of every activity is conformity to the corresponding state of character." Aristotle, "ETHICA NICOMACHEA," in *The Works of Aristotle*, vol. 9. This "conformity to the corresponding state."

22. This is a name that was identified with God's temple in 1 Chron 16:29. Charnock references this passage about 12 different times.

23. Charnock, "A Discourse upon the Holiness of God," in *Works*, 2:269.

24. Charnock, "A Discourse upon the Holiness of God," in *Works*, 2:269.

identified in a soul's beauty which is directly defined by God's holiness, a principle of holiness, and it is incomparable to any other thing in reality that might ascribe the title of beauty. This intrinsic aspect of beauty grounded in holiness is summed up by Thomas Brooks in his discourse on *The Necessity, Excellency, Rarity, and Beauty of Holiness*, "If all natural and artificial beauty were contracted into one beauty," says Brooks, "yet it would be but an obscure and an unlovely beauty to that beauty that holiness puts upon us."[25] It is an implicit aspect built into the very notion of beauty's existence: in God, there is a conjoining of both beauty and holiness, and one does not exist without the other. It is the casting nature of God's holiness that adorns a creature, and "nothing beautifies and bespangles a man like holiness."[26]

i. Nature of Conformity

It was noted above that Charnock identifies the truth of the Christian religion as the conformity of the creature to the imitable perfections of the Creator. That is, this "conformity to him" not only functions as an interpretative grid— "discovery of the God's holiness"—for Charnock's works, but it also speaks to the totality of man's temporal and eternal realm, which obligates the creature to be conformed to that holiness of God. For example, whether Charnock addresses God's existence and attributes, regeneration, knowledge of God, the being of God, or God's holiness, in each *Discourse*, he draws out the profound and substantial reality of who God is. Not only whom God is but that God is and what God is, while at the same time exposing all the various sides of man's existence as a dependent creature. As a result, Charnock intentionally and consistently ushers man to the edge of his creaturely existence in order to establish the foundation for his intrinsic relation to God as his Creator.

This backdrop of the Creator-creature relationship establishes the limited capacity of man's metaphysical, epistemological, and ethical environment. In addition, it further illustrates the covenantal relational reality that God has placed man within; that is, the entirety of man's environment serves to point man to his relational standing with God. This relational aspect of reality is foundational in our understanding of God, and recognizing the primary pillar of scriptural metaphysics. One of the

---

25. Brooks, *The Complete Works of Thomas Brooks*, 4:171.

26. Brooks, "The Necessity, Excellency, Rarity, and Beauty of Holiness," in *Works*, 4:172.

most explicit statements of this reality is set forth by Charnock in *A Discourse upon God's Dominion*,

> The sovereignty of God naturally ariseth from the relation of all things to himself as their entire creator, and their natural and inseparable dependence upon him regarding their being and well-being. It depends not upon the election of men; God hath a natural dominion over us as creatures, before he hath a dominion by consent over us as converts. As soon as ever anything began to be a creature, it was a vassal to God as a lord.[27]

This sovereignty of God is the foundation of the totality of man's reality construct, whether it is considered in the sustaining of his every breath (Acts 17:28) or the bringing forth life from that which is dead. If there is a failure of adequately identifying a sound scriptural metaphysics, we are sure to veer from a proper perspective of whatever else may pertain to the whole of man and his environment (metaphysically, epistemologically, and ethically). That is, if the construct of man's position within creation were anything other than what it is, then the remaining aspects of reality in its entirety would seem to be a moot point of no necessary consideration of who God is in relation to man.

Also, in establishing who God is, Charnock has set the tone and scripturally framed the boundaries for the totality of man's environment and his standing before the Creator as a creature in his Creator-creature relationship. The reality of this relational strand within the disposition of the soul, which cannot be removed, is a necessary component for the existence of the soul because the alternative is non-being. In either case, there is no such thing as an autonomous decision to be made on behalf of the soul; instead, it is intrinsic within its very nature to stand in relation to God. "He is the sovereign Lord, as he is the almighty Creator. The relation of an entire Creator," says Charnock, "induceth the relation of an absolute

---

27. Charnock, "A Discourse upon God's Dominion," in *Works*, 2:411. Charnock's metaphysical foundation is one that is derived from Scripture and done so with a great deal of detail, especially when his two volumes on *The Existence and Attributes of God* are considered. It is in these two volumes we find Charnock unfolding the various elements of the doctrine of God. He identifies the scriptures speaking of a self-contained God, the counsel of God in created reality, temporal creation as the origin of all the facts of the universe, God's providential control over all created reality including the supernatural, and the miraculous work of the redemption. He, in essence, defines scriptural metaphysics, such as the doctrine of the self-contained God, or what is known as the ontological trinity.

THE STRUCTURE OF CONFORMING REALITY—GOD'S HOLINESS

Lord; he that gives being, life, motion, that is the sole cause of the being of a thing which was before nothing, that had nothing to concur with him, nothing to assist him, but by his sole power commands it to stand up into being, is the unquestionable lord and proprietor of that thing that hath no dependence but upon him."[28]

This "relation of an absolute Lord" is not confined to the physical creation; instead, it is threefold: creature, spiritual, and his glorious kingdom.[29] As a result, no "creature can be made without some law in its nature; if it had not law, it would be created to no purpose, to no regular end."[30] This creational design, according to Charnock, would be "utterly unbecoming an infinite wisdom to create a lawless creature, a creature wholly vain."[31] Is it possible to imagine such a rational creature existing? If so, how could we imagine a rational creature that could possibly exist? It is an absurdity, and it is not possible for such a creature; instead, the dominion is intrinsically stamped in the nature and frame of the creature. Therefore, Charnock concludes, it "is impossible [that] there can be a creature which hath not God for its Lord"[32] and this dominion, more specifically, his "dominion over his church as redeemed, and founded in the covenant of grace."[33]

Does this mean that Charnock is suggesting that lordship is covenantal? Is this to suggest that God's sovereignty is implied in the nature of the covenant? It would appear that we would find an affirmation and a negation of this connection between God's sovereignty and covenant. That is, the whole of God's sovereignty betrays a fundamental part of the covenant in Charnock's theological framework where the totality of this relationship between God as the Creator and man as a creature, and the defining principle of that relationship. For example, for Charnock, the defining principle of that relationship is located in what accurately defines the image of the creature. Indeed, it is "in the image of the blessed God, to be conformed to the divine nature" and in this divine nature "he was conformed to the image of his holiness"[34] which is the soul's highest beauty. Flavel best captures this

---

28. Charnock, "A Discourse upon God's Dominion," in *Works,* 2:411.
29. Charnock, "A Discourse upon God's Dominion," in *Works,* 2:407.
30. Charnock, "A Discourse upon God's Dominion," in *Works,* 2:409.
31. Charnock, "A Discourse upon God's Dominion," in *Works,* 2:409.
32. Charnock, "A Discourse upon God's Dominion," in *Works,* 2:409.
33. Charnock, "A Discourse upon God's Dominion," in *Works,* 2:407.
34. Charnock, "A Discourse upon the Goodness of God," in *Works,* 2:309.

soul's beauty in his sermon on Isa 53:11, Wherein *Four Weighty Ends of Christ's Humiliation Are Opened, and Particularly Applied* when he declares:

> Now, when the guilt and filth of sin are washed off, and the beauty of God put upon the soul in sanctification, O what a beautiful creature is the soul now! So lovely in the eyes of Christ, even in its imperfect holiness, that he saith, Cant. 6:5. "Turn away thine eyes from me, for they have overcome me." So we render it, but the Hebrew [הרהיבני] word signifies, "they have made me proud, or puffed me up." It is a beam of divine glory upon the creature, enamouring the very heart of Christ.[35]

That which is "enamouriong the very heart of Christ," that is, the reality of the beauty in the soul is a manifestation of the scriptural principle of covenantal conformity,[36] which is the reality of God's imitable perfection being impressed upon the soul that by design was and is to reflect the image of God's glory.

How does God's sovereignty relate to this principle of covenantal conformity? To this question, Charnock would reply that the connectivity of the two (sovereignty and covenant) is found in God's goodness, which is the rule of his sovereignty. Charnock's understanding of God's sovereignty is that we get an authentic glimpse of a manifold demonstration of his goodness toward the creature, which is nothing short of the sovereignty of God issuing forth from God's throne. His throne is both "holiness ... [and] it is a 'throne of grace,' Heb. 4:16; a throne encircled with a rainbow; Rev. 4:3, 'in sight like to an emerald'—an emblem of the covenant, that hath the pleasantness of a green colour, delightful to the eye, betokening mercy."[37] So, when we consider the goodness of God that flows from his sovereignty or his sovereignty being directed, if you will, according to the rule of goodness,

---

35. Flavel, *The Whole Works of the Reverend John Flavel*, 1:479.

36. Charnock has the whole of his theological structure anchored in the reality of the covenant. The covenant is a fundamental facet of his theology that provides for a grid of interpretation and functions as a grounding factor for knowledge. The Creator has so constructed the very nature of man's soul that it has interwoven within it a principle of reflection. According to Charnock, "God hath interwoven the notion of his sovereignty in the nature of man, in the noblest and most inward acts of his soul, in that faculty which is most necessary for him in his converse in this world, either with God or man. It is stamped upon the conscience of man, and flashes in his face in every act of self-judgment conscience passes upon a man. Every reflection of conscience implies an obligation of man to some law written in his heart, Rom. 2:15." See Charnock, "A Discourse upon God's Dominion," in *Works*, 2:408.

37. Charnock, "A Discourse upon God's Dominion," in *Works*, 2:421.

we find that the gracious condescension of God to his creature is really another mode of declaring the glory of his sovereignty which is manifested in his goodness toward the creature. This sovereign God did this manifestation in a covenantal way because inherent within "I will be your God," there is the implication that there is "protection, government, and relief, which are all grounded upon sovereignty; that therefore which is our greatest burden will be removed by his sovereign power."[38]

The change suggested in the removal of "our greatest burden," Charnock explains the substance of this reality. "Yea, he hath gone higher by virtue of his sovereignty and changed the whole scene and methods of his government after the fall from king creator to king redeemer."[39] The "scene and methods of his government" is described as follows:

> He hath revoked the law of works as a covenant, released the penalty of it from the believing sinner by transferring it upon the surety, who interposed himself by his own will and divine designation. He hath established another covenant, upon other promises, in a higher root, with greater privileges and easier terms.[40]

The description mentioned above outlines the necessary reality for a fallen creature to be restored to that image that was stripped from him at the point of sin. However, behind that description lays a vital question: how was this reality made possible? Alternatively, perhaps, we could ask, how is it possible for this scene and method to change from such a bleak reality to one of promise? It is in Charnock's response that he takes us to the center of the change in the "scene and methods." That is, "Had not God had this right of sovereignty," he says, "not a man of Adam's posterity could have been blessed; he and they must have lain groaning under the misery of the fall, which had rendered both himself and all in his loins unable to observe the terms in the first covenant."[41] Therefore, it is within the context of God's sovereignty that we see his goodness toward us. It is in God's work of regeneration that we see his works as a sovereign, and he does so with mercy. As sovereign, he does not "oppress us by the greatness of his majesty;" says Charnock; instead, "he enters into covenant with us, and allures us by

---

38. Charnock, "A Discourse upon God's Dominion," in *Works*, 2:481.
39. Charnock, "A Discourse upon God's Dominion," in *Works*, 2:431.
40. Charnock, "A Discourse upon God's Dominion," in *Works*, 2:431.
41. Charnock, "A Discourse upon God's Dominion," in *Works*, 2:431.

the cords of a man, and shews himself as much a merciful as an absolute sovereign"[42] by bringing us into the bond of the covenant.

How is it that Charnock makes this covenantal conformity connection between the Creator and the creature? Although Charnock does not use the phrase "covenantal conformity," it is implied in his understanding of God as a covenantal God and his attribute of holiness. Here we find Charnock fusing the whole of our reality to a covenantal substratum in the Creator God because there is a twofold necessity in Charnock's mind, as it pertains to God, and the two are inseparably linked—covenant and holiness. This necessity, according to Charnock, is found in the fact that God "is a God in covenant . . . he is a holy God," and in some sense, there is an equative nature as it pertains to both. That is, at least, how Charnock will equate them in reference to the reality of holiness with life, which is to suggest that the one cannot exist without the other. For example, in his Discourse *upon the Holiness of God*, he speaks in an equative manner of holiness and life.[43] "It is his very life," says Charnock, "so it is called, Eph. 4:18, 'Alienated from the life of God'; that is, from the holiness of God."[44] The reason for this alienation is directly related to the creature's relational standing with the Creator.

Accordingly, Charnock reasons, we "can only [be] alienated from that which we are bound to imitate . . . 'Be you holy, as I am holy'; no other is proposed as our copy; alienated from that purity of God, which is as much as his life."[45] God would be a dead God, "if he were stripped" of his holiness, "more than by the want of any other perfection." This equative correlation between life and holiness, for Charnock, is identified when God swore by his own life "'As I live, saith the Lord'; so he swears by his holiness as if it were his life, and more his life than any other."[46] The rationale would be as follows, according to Charnock, "Let me not live, or let me not be holy, are all one in his oath. His deity could not outlive the life of his purity.[47]

---

42. Charnock, "A Discourse upon God's Dominion," in *Works*, 2:489.

43. One cannot help but see the continuity in Charnock's thought, especially as it relates to the whole of God's redemptive plan in Christ through the Word and Spirit. The principle of life is equative to the principle of holiness, and the principle of holiness was the very thing ripped from man the moment Adam and Eve entertained thoughts contrary to God.

44. Charnock, "A Discourse upon the Holiness of God," in *Works*, 2:192.

45 Charnock, "A Discourse upon the Holiness of God," in *Works*, 2:192.

46. Charnock, "A Discourse upon the Holiness of God," in *Works*, 2:192.

47. Charnock, "A Discourse upon the Holiness of God," in *Works*, 2:192. This

ii. Reflection of Conformity

It is crucial to keep in mind that Charnock, in all of his efforts, is attempting to grasp that divine beauty that is wrapped up in a soul that has the formation of Christ stamped upon it and the reflection of that imitable perfection of God. That is, he is continuously refining his understanding of the substantive nature that would define the soul's disposition, which would accurately redound this glory. What should describe such glory on the creature's part? For Charnock, there are several descriptors employed that he might convey with vivid imagery that is intrinsically redounding of that glory, which is intrinsically interwoven in the very image that God created man. The theme that runs through them all is the notion of holiness.

Charnock's understanding of God's holiness, which functioned as an interpretative grid, was not a matter of convenience in his thought or theology. Instead, it was an indispensable necessity for the truths of Scripture to be adequately set forth and understood, especially as it pertains to the deforming reality of sin in a soul that was conformed, originally, to the image of God and his holiness. In some sense, the deforming reality of sin becomes an avenue, in Charnock's estimation, for God to convey his grace—better yet, to demonstrate the depths of his grace in creating man, the apex of his creation, in his divine image. Therefore, the notion of the "image of God and his Holiness" is an exciting aspect of the creature's reality that Charnock will grapple with throughout his writings to explore the substance of what is contained in such a notion. It seems that he is always grasping for something further to depict what this "image of God and his Holiness" is.

This grasping is associated with Charnock's wanting to convey and depict, to the extent possible, the reality contained in the imagery of the "image of God." This continuous grasping can be seen in various parts of his discourses, and each one seems to grow more and more graphic of the "image of God." Charnock does use the phrase "image of God;" however, he employs other imagery to convey the substance of that reality in the "image of God." For example, it is the "wise workmanship of God," and the light of God brought it about. "The soul was lighted by God, and created according to the image of God" and, although the notion of the

---

equative notion of life and holiness is further identified in comparison to the difference between the Creator God and the creature. "The holiness of a creature may be reduced into nothing as well as his substance, but the holiness of the Creator cannot be diminished, dimmed, or overshadowed." See Charnock, "A Discourse upon the Holiness of God," in *Works*, 2:296.

A SOUL FRAMED IN CHRIST

image gives us a depiction of this image of God, it is not just an image, but "the exactest image of God under heaven." How does one convey what is meant by the "exactest image of God"? For Charnock, it is found in the Greek words Τι ἄγαλμα Θεοῦ, which translates into "*a statue of God*." He explains this imagery of the "statute of God" as follows: by "the nature of our own souls we may come to some knowledge of the original and copy." Furthermore, he points out, "as we have clearer apprehensions of the sun by the image of it imprinted upon a glass, or other transparent body, than we can have by any other creature, though the image of the sun be much less glorious than the sun itself, whose image it is."[48]

Although, this depiction of the image as the "statute of God" serves to further convey the reality in the soul that God created in his image. For Charnock, it does not seem to have reached a level of satisfaction in conveying the truth of this image because he presses the grasping of this reality. This dissatisfaction can be seen in another approach by Charnock where we find one of the most graceful depictions of his understanding of this glorious reality of the image: "Grace hath its print from God, and is conformity to the holiness of God, as appearing in his law."[49] Here, he touches upon the

---

48. Charnock, "A Discourse of the Knowledge of God in Christ," in *Works*, 4:117.

49. So, when we identify that he employs the word 'grace' some 3,600 times in his writings, can we make a claim that, therefore, 'grace' is a significant component of his theological structure? There is an inherent difficulty with this approach because the number of times a word is used would be arbitrary and contributed to the subject matter of the discourse. For example, in a word count performed on *A Discourse upon the Holiness of God*, we find the word 'holy' or 'holiness' used 628 times; however, this number should not surprise us considering the subject matter of this discourse, and we would anticipate a high concentration of 'holy' or 'holiness.' Perhaps, to better understand a fundamental concept that has a defining essence to his theology requires us to narrow down the word count, such as, the word 'holy' or 'holiness' in his volume on regeneration. In volume 3, the word 'holy' or 'holiness' is used some 571 times in the whole of volume 3, compared to 628 in *A Discourse upon the Holiness of God*. However, it is interesting to note that the second-highest concentrated use of 'holy' or 'holiness' is found in volume 3; more specifically, it is used 164 times in *A Discourse of God's Being the Author of Reconciliation*, which is his sermon on 2 Cor 5:18–19. As noted earlier, the total word count for 'grace' is approximately 3,600 times, and the highest concentration of that word is found in volume 3. In volume 3, the highest usage in Charnock's *Discourse of the Efficient of Regeneration: Part I and II* (583 times) and *Discourse of God's Being the Author of Reconciliation* (255 times). It quickly jumps out that the words 'holy,' 'holiness,' and 'grace' have a good deal of usage throughout his writings; however, we find a high concentration of usage with both terms (grace and holiness) in a similar discourse: *Discourse of God's Being the Author of Reconciliation*. As an operational backdrop to Charnock's understanding of this 'holiness' and 'grace,' we find him placing it within the covenantal environment that provides for the true meaning, which is only found in God who is covenantal in all of his

kernel of our existence and the very manner that God created the soul to redound and reflect that glorious image of His holiness. This printing by God's grace brings about conformity to the imitable perfections of God's holiness. Charnock continues to elaborate on this grace, which has its print from God. "It is the image of God;" he says, "there is an harmony and proportion of all graces in the soul to those perfections of holiness which are in God, as there is of the members of the body of a child to its father; in respect of this likeness men are said to be the children of God."[50]

It would seem, to most at least, that Charnock has captured the substance of that image of God in the "harmony and proportion of all graces . . . perfections of holiness." However, there still seems to be more to be added to this understanding of the image of God that has been stamped on the soul. In this depiction of the image, Charnock finds himself borrowing from the heathens and transposing a heathen's descriptor of the soul to that of God's grace. "It may be better said of grace," notes Charnock, "than it was said of the soul by the heathen, *Scintilla divinæ essentiæ*, or, as the Jews say, souls were the shavings or chips of the throne of glory."[51] Graces are the drops of God's perfections in that they are so exact an image of him. However, to avoid an accusation of participatory metaphysics, Charnock does clarify his understanding of this partaking of the divine nature. It is not "that God bestows anything of the divine essence upon the soul," says Charnock, "but an image and representation of himself, just as a golden seal conveys to the wax the image engraven on it, but not the least particle of its matter, the wax remaining wax, though under another form and figure."[52]

Although, to some extent, Charnock does seek to exhaust this imagery of the image of God, at the end of his searching for a means to convey the reality of this glorious image of God's holiness, he concludes that the substance contained in this image of God's holiness, his imitable perfections, is identified in the likeness to God. "This likeness is a likeness to God in his highest perfection," Charnock says, "his holiness, which runs through all, and may be applied to all the attributes, as holy power, &c., and herein grace excels the perfections of the whole creation put together, for

---

dealings. Hence, the reason we find Charnock using the term 'covenant' or 'covenant of redemption' approximately 300 times in that same *Discourse of God's Being the Author of Reconciliation*. This word mapping depicts the webbing of Charnock's thoughts, especially as it pertains to God's redemptive work.

50. Charnock, "A Discourse Proving Weak Grace Victorious," in *Works*, 5:229.
51. Charnock, "A Discourse Proving Weak Grace Victorious," in *Works*, 5:295.
52. Charnock, "A Discourse Proving Weak Grace Victorious," in *Works*, 5:295.

all the creatures are not so like to God as grace makes the soul."⁵³ Therefore, this image of God speaks to the pervasive nature of God's grace in working a new reality in the soul of man, framing a new reality in the soul through the redemptive work of Christ.

b. Conclusion

Therefore, the sum and substance of the reality are found in the new creature; that is, Charnock captures the soul's ultimate object of conformity in *A Discourse upon the Holiness of God*. "Conformity to God was man's original happiness in his created state," says Charnock,

> and what was naturally so, cannot but be immutably so in its own nature. The beauty of every copied thing consists in its likeness to the original; everything hath more of loveliness, as it hath greater impressions of its first pattern; in this regard holiness hath more of beauty on it, than the whole creation, because it partakes of a greater excellency of God than the sun, moon, and stars. No greater glory can be, than to be a conspicuous and visible image of the invisible, and holy, and blessed God.⁵⁴

This conformity to holiness is what John Owen (1620–1680) described as being the "honour of our souls,"⁵⁵ and the more holiness that is ascribed to it, the more honor is to accompany it. "Holiness consists in our conformity to God," says Watson, "holiness is the sparkling of the divine nature, a beam of God shining in the soul."⁵⁶ The very nature of "holiness implieth a conformity to God"⁵⁷ and in this conformity, "we are beautified with holiness,"⁵⁸ observes Thomas Manton (1620–1677), and it the

---

53. Charnock, "A Discourse Proving Weak Grace Victorious," in *Works*, 5:229.

54. Charnock, "A Discourse upon the Holiness of God," in *Works*, 2:269. The association of holiness and happiness speaks further to the communion and fellowship that was inherently designed in God, creating man in his image as a rational creature. The two—happiness and holiness—are intrinsically linked together. George Swinnock states: "The holiness and happiness of the rational creature consisteth in these two: his holiness, in conformity to God; his happiness, in communion with him. And these two have a dependence on each other." See Swinnock, *The Works of George Swinnock*, 4:376.

55. Owen, *The Works of John Owen*, 3:430.

56. Watson, *The Select Works of the Rev. Thomas Watson*, 598.

57. Manton, *The Complete Works of Thomas Manton*, 6:49.

58. Manton, "Sermons upon John 17, Sermon 1," in *Works*, 10:413.

completeness of conformity to that holiness is the "great thing that God designeth," says Thomas Boston, and it entails "the whole man."[59]

Undeniably, it is the greatest bespangling of the soul, if you will, when the attribute of God's holiness is the defining principle of God's created image. "What can be more attractive of our imitation," Charnock asks, "than that which is the original of all purity, holiness? Although there is beauty found in the fact that we are creatures fashioned by the hand of the Creator, yet the greater beauty that excellency is found in "having a stamp of God upon us."[60] Yet, this brings us to the crux of the problem. The very thing that defined the highest excellence of man, that great beauty of holiness that was far greater than the creation of the body and the soul's faculties, is "greater than the creation of the whole world because it was God's attribute that was stamped upon the soul. However, [it] has found its beauty defaced by sin."[61] Not only does "sin . . . deface its beauty," contends Flavel, but sin "razed out the Divine image which was its glory, and stamped the image of Satan upon it; turned all its noble powers an faculties again the author and fountain of its being."[62]

For the first time, the notion of conformity was to be known from a perspective that was foreign to man's existence. That is, conformity would now stand in contrast to deformity. All the principles of the repository in the mind would find themselves standing in a relation of contrariety, a contrariety that became the principle to replace holiness. According to Charnock,

> The essential faculties of the rational soul: the mind, the repository of principles, the faculty whereby we should judge of things honest or dishonest; the understanding, the discursive faculty and the reducer of those principles into practical dictates,—that part whereby we reason and collect one thing from another, framing conclusions from the principles in the mind; the heart, *i.e.* the will, conscience, affections, which were to apply those principles, draw out those reasonings upon the stage of the life, all corrupted,—one vain, the other dark, and the third stark blind.[63]

---

59. Boston, *The Whole Works of Thomas Boston: Sermons*, 4:67–72.
60. Charnock, "A Discourse upon the Holiness of God," in *Works*, 2:270.
61. Charnock, "A Discourse of the Efficient of Regeneration," in *Works*, 3:194.
62. Flavel, *The Whole Works of the Reverend John Flavel*, 2:539.
63. Charnock, "A Discourse of the Knowledge of God," in *Works*, 4:73. Interestingly, with no citation, these exact words appear in Thomas Boston's sermon on Acts 3:22, *Of Christ's Prophetical Office*. "All the essential faculties of the rational soul are entirely

The full extent of this deforming principle of reality, the contrariety, will be considered in greater detail under the section entitled *The Frayed Strands of the Soul's Disposition*, specifically what Charnock identifies as the principle of contrariety. It is mentioned here that we might establish the nature of the relational standing of the creature before the Creator with a change in disposition. Unfortunately, we have "departed from our original pattern"; Charnock says, "we were created to live the life of God, that is, a life of holiness, but now we are 'alienated from the life of God,' Eph. 4:18; and of a beautiful piece we are become deformed, daubed over with the most defiling mud."[64] And the resultant reality is that the soul's conformity has been frayed.

---

corrupted; the mind which is the repository of principles, that noble faculty, whereby we judge of things good and evil; the understanding, that discursive faculty, whereby we collect one thing from another, framing conclusions from the principles of the mind, and reducing these principles into practical dictates; and the heart, i.e. the will, conscience, and affections, which were to apply these principles, and draw out these reasonings on the stage of life; all are corrupted." See Boston, *The Whole Works of Thomas Boston*, 1:425.

64. Charnock, "A Discourse upon the Holiness of God," in *Works,* 2:250.

III

Fraying the Strands of Conformity

a. Principle of Contrariety

IN LIGHT OF THE previous section dealing with the reality of holiness as it pertains to God and his relational standing with his creatures, it is only proper that we transition to consider man's condition as it pertains to this holiness of God considering his fallen state of existence. If we fail to grasp the true nature, properties, and effects of this fallen state of man, then we are sure to fail to apply the proper remedy to his condition.

How fundamental is a scriptural understanding of man's depravity and the implications of this depraved reality on the totality of man's existence, as well as to a proper understanding of fundamental doctrines of Christianity?[1] What content or substance would be found in the reality of man's depravity if there is no real perception of the sum and substance of God's holiness? That is, can we have a proper view of sin that fails to account for God's holiness? To what extent can we grasp the gravity of our condition if we are never brought, in our depravity, before a holy Creator? In these questions and many more, we find the scriptural grounding of Charnock's thought in establishing the intrinsic relation of the Creator-creature and the necessity of conformity. The attribute of God's holiness is an essential attribute of God and the creature that was formed in his image. Hence, when the bands of the creature's conformity to the holy

---

1. This period that is identified as the period of High Orthodoxy (1640–1700) was no stranger to the various doctrinal understanding of man's condition after the fall in the Garden.

Creator were ethically severed, all of the creature's thoughts, words, and deeds were defined by depravity, and "all sin," says Charnock, "is against this [holiness] attribute, all sin aims in general at the being of God, but in particular at the holiness of his being."[2]

In his work, *Spiritual Life Delineated*, Thomas Watson opens Section XXVI by pointing out this very reality. "How different is sin viewed as we are sinners or saints: as we are in the covenant of mercy or out of it: how difficult is it to get right views of our own depravity; surely there are depths of iniquity, as well as deep things of God."[3] In these words, Watson captures the fundamental necessity of the doctrine outlined in the *Canons of Dort*, more specifically, the doctrine of man's depravity. Watson rightly identifies the necessity of setting forth this doctrine as the difficulty to obtain the correct views of our depravity. We can go even further with Watson and suggest that it is not only challenging to get "right views of our own depravity" but how much more the need to comprehend God's view of our depravity. It is here that we see the glaring contrariety between God's holiness as depicted in the previous section and man's depraved condition where holiness has been stricken from his image. This necessity to obtain a right view of our depravity is an understanding that is consistently present throughout Charnock's discourses, and we find him exposing this depravity of the soul's nature as it stands in contrariety to God's holiness.

---

2. Charnock, "A Discourse upon the Holiness of God," in *Works*, 2:243. The emphasis on God's holiness is an attribute that transcends the other attributes, hence, one that affects all the others. Peter Van Mastricht makes the same distinction about this particular attribute of holiness. "And (5) not so much as a certain particular attribute of his," says Mastricht, "but as a universal affection, affecting, as it were, every other attribute of his, and thus his power, or his arm, is called holy (Isa. 52:10; etc.)." Mastricht further notes that this attribute is "not some common affection of his, but the one that is chief by far, the one by which he is celebrated even by the angels themselves, not once, but three times and in the same breath, as it were: Holy, holy, holy is Jehovah Sabaoth" (Isa. 6:3; Rev. 4:8), which is nowhere read regarding any other attribute of his." See Van Mastricht, *Theoretical-Practical Theology: Faith in the Triune God*, vol. 2. Charnock expresses the very same thing. According to Charnock, "If any, this attribute hath an excellency above his other perfections. There are some attributes of God we prefer, because of our interest in them, and the relation they bear to us; as we esteem his goodness before his power, and his mercy, whereby he relieves us, before his justice, whereby he punisheth us. As there are some we more delight in because of the goodness we receive by them, so there are some that God delights to honour because of their excellency . . . Where do you find any other attribute trebled in the praises of it, as this? Isa. 6:3, 'Holy, holy, holy is the Lord of hosts; the whole earth is full of his glory.'" See Charnock, "A Discourse upon the Holiness of God," in *Works*, 2:191.

3. Watson, *Spiritual Life Delineated*, 207.

Throughout *Attributes and the Existence of God,* Charnock continually provides an exposition of what the scriptures have revealed about the attributes of God. He then moves from those attributes and quickly draws man to the center of that reality to account for his willful defection from God. As a result of this defection from God, the entirety of man's reality has been re-framed by what Charnock identifies as the "principle of contrariety" that stands in direct opposition to the image of holiness and the Creator of that image. "All sin is a violence to this perfection. There is not an iniquity in the world, but directs its venomous sting against the divine purity,"[4] says Charnock. Furthermore, he describes what is contained in this universal nature of iniquity: secret wickedness against God's omniscience; distrust against his providence; unbelief against his mercy; censuring against his wisdom; fear of men rather than God; dismissing his truth, his promises, his wrath. It is here that we see the universality of iniquity in the soul, "all agree together," notes Charnock, "in their enmity against this, which is the peculiar glory [holiness] of the Deity."[5] "Every one of them," Charnock continues, "is a receding from the divine image, and the blackness of every one is the deeper, by how much the distance of it from the holiness of God is the greater."[6] This great distance discloses the nature of the fallen creature and exposes the fact that the principle of holiness has been supplanted by a principle of contrariety, more specifically, the principle of "contrariety to the holiness of God,"[7] which Charnock identifies as "the cause of all the absolute atheism (if there be any such) in the world."[8]

   4. Charnock, "A Discourse upon the Holiness of God," in *Works,* 2:243.
   5. Charnock, "A Discourse upon the Holiness of God," in *Works,* 2:243.
   6. Charnock, "A Discourse upon the Holiness of God," in *Works,* 2:243.
   7. Charnock, "A Discourse upon the Holiness of God," in *Works,* 2:243.
   8. Charnock, "A Discourse upon the Holiness of God," in *Works,* 2:243. This qualifying statement of atheism should be considered in the context of Charnock's discourse on the "Existence of God," a sermon on Ps 14:1 "The fool hath said in his heart, there is no God." He refers to Cocceius's distinction of atheism. That is, he presents a "threefold denial of God." "There is a threefold denial of God. 1. *Quoad existentiam,* this is absolute atheism. 2. *Quoad providentiam,* or his inspection into, or care of the things of the world, bounding him in the heavens. 3. *Quoad naturam,* in regard of one or other of the perfections due to his nature." See Charnock, "The Existence of God," in *Works,* 1:127. Once again, we find continuity in Charnock's system of thought, and each discourse is another strand or thread that is being intertwined with the whole of his theological framework. That is, God is holy, and he shaped man in conformity to that holiness when he created man in his image. As a result of sin, the principle of holiness, that conformity to the Creator, has been replaced with another principle, and conformity to the Creator has been replaced with deformity.

Although it would not seem possible to surpass the existence of "absolute atheism" in terms of rejecting the holiness of God; however, for Charnock, "absolute atheism" is not the outer edge of contrariety to God's holiness. Instead, according to Charnock, "debasing the Creator to be a creature of their own fancies . . . fashioning him not according to that beautiful image he impressed upon them by creation . . . this is worse than idolatry."[9] Therefore, what we see in Charnock identifying the principle of contrariety is an attempt to get the right view of depravity. Charnock concludes that such a contrariety to God's holiness is actually "worse than absolute atheism or denial of God."[10] This "worse than" reality is depicted by George Swinnock in his meditation of the sinfulness of sin; it suggests that we consider the sum and substance of sin in the following framework:

> In its nature; its contrariety to God, his being, his law, his honour; its opposition to our own souls, their present purity and peace, their future glory and bliss. In its causes; Satan, the wicked one, its father, the corrupt heart of man its mother. In its properties; how defiling it is, filthiness itself; how infectious it is, overspreading the whole man, polluting all his natural, civil, spiritual actions, and making his praying, hearing, singing, an abomination; how deceiving it is, pretending meat, and intending murder. In its effects; the curse of God on all the creatures, evident by the vanity in them, the vexation they bring with them; in the anger of God on sinners, apparent in those temporal punishments, spiritual judgments, and eternal torments which he inflicteth on them.[11]

Swinnock was echoing Charnock's perspective in his consideration of the devastating reality contained in this principle of contrariety, especially in seizing the soul and supplanting the principle of holiness. Swinnock's frame of reference is an effort to give an orientation of the pervasiveness of depravity: its nature, its causes, its properties, and its effects. If such a principle of contrariety to God's holiness is the defining principle of a depraved soul, we should endeavor to view our depravity from God's perspective, precisely the nature, scope, and effects of that principle of contrariety.

---

9. Charnock, "Practical Atheism," in *Works*, 1:243.
10. Charnock, "Practical Atheism," in *Works*, 1:243.
11. Swinnock, *The Works of George Swinnock*, 2:427.

i. Nature of Contrariety

This principle of contrariety is not localized to one particular aspect of man's soul (i.e., contrariety in the affections); instead, "it is natural, it is also universal," because "a natural man," says Charnock, "is in a state of universal contrariety."[12] The universal nature of sin is a poison that infiltrates the entirety of human nature,[13] it is a "universal infection, 'a lake of Sodom' in every man's nature."[14] It is all-encompassing, by its very nature, and it is a notion that Charnock employs to capture the depravity of man.[15] We get the reach of this contrariety when Charnock points out that every sin stands in direct "contrariety to the law, sovereignty, work, glory, yea, the very being of God."[16] This principle of contrariety is a principle of sin, and sin "is the contagion of the soul," declares Charnock, "the universal stain of nature; nothing but pollution succeeded in the place of original purity."[17] We find the concept of "contrariety to God" echoed by other men of this period. For example, Thomas Brooks in *The Necessity, Excellency, Rarity, and Beauty of Holiness*. In that discourse, Brooks brings his readers to face the full-frontal reality of their sin, that is, the fullness of the contrariety to God, which is identified in their unholiness. Consider his, somewhat, comprehensive description of man's contrariety to God: "Their

---

12. Charnock, "Man's Enmity against God," in *Works*, 5:464.

13. Charnock, "A Discourse upon the Holiness of God," in *Works*, 2:216.

14. Charnock, "A Discourse upon the Holiness of God," in *Works*, 2:227.

15. This notion of a "principle of contrariety" is Charnock's way of drawing out the fullness of the spiritual reality that came into existence when Adam and Eve took of the fruit of the tree. That is, there was a principle of holiness, a principle of conforming to holiness that God had created man, when he said, "Let Us make man in our image." However, this principle of conformity to God's holiness was uprooted, and a new principle took its place, and this is what Charnock identifies as the principle of contrariety, which is his way of depicting the kernel aspect of reality and what took place within the soul when holiness was replaced by depravity. This particular principle of contrariety is unique to Charnock and is not used by others during this period. However, we do find the content of this notion expressed by Thomas Brooks, Thomas Manton, William Bates, George Swinnock, John Owen, and Thomas Goodwin.

16. Charnock, "A Discourse of the Pardon of Sin," in *Works*, 5:439. The phrase, "contrariety to . . . the very being of God," is intentional and significant phrase because it adheres consistently with his perspective of sin that has an implicit aspect of hate directed toward God. The irony is that the very sinful wishful thinking within man's heart is nothing short of a request to cease to exist or have himself come into non-being. This principle of contrariety will be developed in another section of this paper.

17. Charnock, "A Discourse of the Efficient of Regeneration," in *Works*, 3:195.

natures, principles, practices, aims, minds, wills, affections, judgments, intentions, and resolutions," says Brooks, "are contrary to God, his name, nature, being, truth, and glory."[18] As if this imagery was not sufficient, he continues to draw out the reality of the soul's contrariety to God's holiness, which depicts the depths of this principle in the soul's depravity. The contrariety speaks to the polarization between God's holiness and the soul's defining principle of depravity; that is, according to Brooks, you "may as soon bring east and west, north and south, light and darkness, heaven and hell together, as you shall bring a holy God and unholy souls together . . . that unholy persons are made up of contrarieties to God."[19]

The reality of the creature being identified in this contrariety to the Creator is accompanied by a host of issues for the creature. For example, Thomas Manton points out that there is an inherent aspect of contrariety, and these contraries surface in any contrariety of the creature to the Creator, especially when it places the creature in a bizarre predicament that pushes the edges of his existence in the presence of God. Manton points out that the position of contrariety equates to the position of "a creature who is nothing." "There is an eternal God against a poor creature whose breath is in his nostrils," declares Manton, "a God who is all in all, and a creature who is nothing."[20] The nature of nothingness, according to Manton, is threefold concerning the Creator and the creature: contrariety, comparison, and exclusion. He describes it accordingly:

> Nothing in opposition or contrariety to God or his people: Isa. 41:11, 'Behold, they that are incensed against thee shall be as nothing.' Nothing in comparison with God: Isa. 40:17, 'All nations before him are as nothing; they are accounted less than nothing and vanity;' Dan. 4:35, 'The inhabitants of the earth are reputed before him as nothing.' Nothing by way of exclusion of God; as the sunbeam is. nothing when the sun withdraweth, or the sound is nothing when the musician taketh away his mouth from the pipe or instrument: 'Thou takest away their breath; and they die.'[21]

---

18. Brooks, "The Necessity, Excellency, Rarity, and Beauty of Holiness," in *Works*, 4:53. See Lev 26:21–24, 27–28, 40–41; Isa 58:4–6; Jer 44:16–18; 2:25, and 18:11–12.

19. Brooks, "The Necessity, Excellency, Rarity, and Beauty of Holiness," in *Works*, 4:53.

20. Manton, *The Complete Works of Thomas Manton*, 18:279.

21. Manton, "Sermon upon 2 Corinthians IV. 18," in *Works*, 18:279.

No doubt, the notion of nothingness is consistently threaded through the Puritans' works, especially when man, as the creature, is brought into the presence of God. Even more so when that creature "is in a state of universal contrariety."[22] Therefore, the depraved man stands in his sin, and sin "stands in a contrariety unto God." "It is a rebellion against his sovereignty," Owen says, "an opposition to his holiness, a provocation to his justice, a rejection of his yoke, a casting off, what lies in the sinner, of that dependence which a creature hath on its Creator."[23] Therefore, in essence, the very existence of this "principle of contrariety" establishes a foreign dialect in the heart that is consistent with their "διαλογισμοὶ, their reasonings," says Charnock, [which] became empty and contradictory; [because] their primitive light departed, and darkness, as a privation, took place."[24] And such dark reasoning consists of the following language: "Depart from us, for we do not desire the knowledge of Your ways,"[25] nor your holiness.

This notion of departure conveys the substance of contrariety that Charnock has identified with the depravity of man. Boston elaborates upon that departure in his sermon on Hebrews 11:28, "*The Best Security against the Day of Wrath.*" In his sermon, Boston, like Charnock in his sermon on Rom 8:7, is addressing the enmity of a depraved soul against God. In doing so, Boston identifies the principle of contrariety as well, and he designates it as "a downright contrariety" that is inherent in the depraved nature. "There is a bending away from God," Boston says, "who originally was, and of right is our chief end, Psalm 14:3, Jer. 2:13." This "bending away" is a manifestation of contrariety in the realm of the soul, that is, the "heart of man," Boston continues, "has not only left its rest in God, but is filled with natural enmity against him," referencing the text of Charnock's sermon on Rom 8:7. So, this "bending away" is the utter dislike of that which is holy and of God's law, which is a transcript of God's holiness. Therefore, Boston concludes, "There is a downright contrariety in his nature against the nature of God, and in his will against the will of God . . . bent towards the creature as the chief good, in the room of God, Jer. 2:13." Hence the natural voice of the heart in man is, "Who will shew us any good?" Psalm 4:6."[26]

---

22. Charnock, "Man in Enmity against God," in *Works*, 5:464.
23. Owen, *The Works of John Owen*, 6:399.
24. Charnock, "A Discourse of the Efficient of Regeneration," in *Works*, 3:185.
25. Job 21:14 KJV.
26. Boston, "The Best Security against the Day of Wrath," in *Works*, 10:335.

For Charnock, this "bending away" is also a manifestation of the rebellion, which comes about in various ways. However, as Boston noted, the foundation of this rebellion is a matter of hatred toward the Creator. According to Edward Veel, Charnock depicts this hatred in his sermon on Rom 8:7, *Man's Enmity to God*. In this sermon, he sets forth "an excellent portraiture of the old man; a graphical description of the devil's image[27] impressed upon and deforming the most beautiful part of this lower creation." By definition, a 'portrait' is a painting, a sculpture, or an artistic representation of a person with the intent to display the semblance or personality of a person, emphasizing the face of the person looking directly at the one painting the portrait.[28] It is, in some sense, face-to-face.

In this sermon, *Man's Enmity to God*, Charnock is merely echoing the words of the *Canons of Dort*, which states that man is "rebelling against God at the devil's instigation, and by his own free will, he deprived himself." It is essential to point out that the *Canons* first identifies this depraved reality in the context of "rebelling against God" and the resultant nature of this rebellious reality. This rebellion opens up the realm of our depravity that, according to the *Canons*, manifests itself in "blindness, terrible darkness, futility, and distortion of judgment in his *mind*; perversity, defiance, and hardness in his *heart* and *will*; and finally, impurity in all his *emotions*" [emphasis mine].[29] The exacting and comprehensive measure—the totality—of rebellion could not have been framed in a more precise manner than the words penned in the *Canons of Dort*.

---

ii. Effects of Contrariety[30]

This "totality" can take on various meanings, and it appears that the *Canons* have covered their bases when they put forth their understanding of

---

27. This notion of the "devil's image" is strong language, yet it is consistent with these reformed men to identify man's loss of God's image and replace it with the image of the devil.

28 *Merriam-Webster's Collegiate Dictionary.*

29. *Canons of Dort* 1619, Chapter 1, Article 1.

30. There is a great deal of history with this concept of man and the impact of sin. You have the Roman Catholics who did not hold to any intellectual impact from sin. Evangelicals that suggest there is a type of cooperation that takes place between God and man; that is, man can choose between serving God the Creator or the creature. Less—consistent Calvinism, which suggests that man is depraved but not willing to go as far as to say that the totality of man is depraved. The less—consistent Calvinism

the Holy Scripture about man's depraved state of existence. For example, we could say that "totality" takes the form of man's relationship with God (ethical orientation–alienated), which is indicative of the rebellion and manifests the reality rooted in the heart. More specifically, the alienation "from God's life, i.e., from an imitation of his life, as well as animation by a living principle contrary to him, [which] is rooted in the 'blindness of the heart,"[31] says Charnock.

It is the wording found in the *Canons* that further reveals what Charnock has in mind about his principle of contrariety, specifically the universality of that contrariety.[32] For example, the "totality" of total depravity takes on the form of self (subjective, internal thoughts and intentions of man[33]), which the *Canons* describe as man "brought upon himself blindness, terrible darkness, futility, and distortion of judgment in his *mind*; perversity, defiance, and hardness in his *heart* and *will*; and finally, impurity in all his *emotions*."[34] "Totality" takes the form of man that is made in the

---

appears to approach the Roman Catholic position about the capacity of reason in man. Finally, there are the Reformed Calvinist who believes that every aspect of the soul has been tainted by sin and the sinful implications are worked out in their intellect, mind, heart, will, emotions, and affections. This Reformed concept is defined within the structure of the Creator-creature distinction and the fact that God is man's ultimate environment. So, any suggestion to escape this environment is nothing short of a man attempting to "slip into nonbeing."

31. Charnock, "A Discourse of the Knowledge of God," in *Works*, 4:29.

32. Although this is somewhat simplified, the nature of adequately identifying man's depraved state was one of the critical components that sparked the *Canons of Dort* in its efforts to offer up a scriptural response to the doctrine that the Remonstrants held to be true. It would be in the period that followed, identified as high orthodoxy (1620–1700), that the *Canons* would generate a significant number of writings on the doctrine of regeneration. Some postulate that the entirety of the doctrine of regeneration was the focus or the primary concern of the Synod of Dort, not to mention the influence on the following generation of theologians. See Citron, *New Birth: A Study of the Evangelical Doctrine of Conversation in the Protestant Fathers*, 27. See Toon, *Born Again*, 124. According to Toon, "The teaching of the Synod of Dort had an important influence on the development of the Reformed tradition and fixed the way in which the doctrine of regeneration would be taught in those churches for the next two or three centuries." See also, Van Den Berg, *The Synod of Dort in the Balance*, 176–94, or Wright, "Regeneration and Redemptive History," 52–67. It should be noted that "high orthodoxy," notes Richard Muller, "did not create the Reformed doctrinal system; it modified, developed, and elaborated an extant system in relation to a changing intellectual environment." See, finally, Muller, *Post-Reformation Reformed Dogmatics*, 1:74.

33. This is the only sermon published by Charnock while he was alive. See Charnock, "The Sinfulness and Cure of Thoughts," in *Works*, 5:287–316.

34 *Canons of Dort* 1619, Chapter 3, Article 3.

image of God, which is not distorted. This "totality" entails the multi-relational concept of man with man, as noted by the *Canons*, that "all people are conceived in sin and are born children of wrath."[35] It is in accordance with this wrath that Charnock notes that nothing "is the meritorious cause of God's wrath, but sin."[36] So, in this sense, the impact of sin in the expression "total depravity" pursuing all the types of "coherence" (relationships, connections, intertwinements, and so forth) between sin and man, and how the "totality" of man has been racked with sin and the implications of this depravity manifesting itself.

This type of "totality" brings to mind the totality of the faculties that find their unity in the substratum of principles— "universal contrariety"—that they are grounded in depravity. The intellect, mind, heart, will, emotions, and affections are united; and each faculty has been pervasively impacted by sin. There are only two states of existence that will find this unity in the totality of man's being. The first is in his depravity because all aspects of man's existence are operating within the realm of depravity. Second, if there is a gracious act of regeneration that God works through his Word and Spirit; then this unity that is found in the totality of man's innermost man is disrupted. This act of regeneration produces a new substratum of principles, and this unity that was rooted in depravity unravels, and a new substratum of principles (holiness, righteousness, and true knowledge) are infused, which completely redirects the totality of the soul. This new substratum of principles; however, causes a contrariety in man because the new creature in Christ has a new object that captures the focus and direction of the soul. According to Peter Van Mastricht, there is an "implantation of a principle or substratum of holy exercises in regeneration is argued and known from its exercises, and operations."[37]

Nonetheless, the *Canons* speak in an exact language when describing this condition of the human in his fallen state, Chapter 3, Article 1 and Article 3,

> However, rebelling against God at the devil's instigation and by his own free will, he deprived himself of these outstanding gifts. Instead, in their place he brought upon himself blindness, terrible darkness, futility, and distortion of judgment in his *mind*; perversity, defiance, and hardness in his *heart* and *will*; and

---

35 *Canons of Dort* 1619, Chapter 3, Article 3.
36 Charnock, "The Sinfulness and Cure of Thoughts," in *Works*, 5:40.
37 Mastricht, *A Treatise on Regeneration*, 19 n.

finally impurity in all his *emotions*" [emphasis mine] (Art. 1). "Therefore, all people are conceived in sin and are born children of wrath, unfit for any saving good, inclined to evil, dead in their sins, and slaves to sin . . . they are neither willing nor able to return to God, to reform their distorted nature, or even to dispose themselves to such reform (Art. 3).[38]

The potential for ambiguity in identifying what "total" means is removed with the words employed by the framers of the *Canons*, where "totality" of depravity can be spoken of in an all-inclusive manner. The following words and phrases are used to describe man's fallen depraved state: "blindness," "darkness," "futility and distortion," "perversity," "defiance," "hardness," "impurity," "all people conceived in sin," "born children of wrath," "unfit," "inclined to evil," "dead," "slaves," "neither willing nor able to," and "distorted nature." This picture painted of man's fallen state, his nature, is not a perspective that the *Canons of Dort* pulled out of thin air, nor does it exist in a vacuum; instead, this reality of man's "total" inability is squarely rooted in Scripture. For example, Gen 6:5 gives a dim perspective of man and states that "the wickedness of man was great in the earth, and that every intent of the thoughts of his heart was only evil continually."[39] However, the content of this verse does prompt some questions about the language used. For example, are we to believe that man is incapable of thinking any thought that is not assigned to intentional evil? That is, is a man capable, in this state of existence, to produce a thought that would be untethered from the evil that is within in his heart? If so, how does he untether such thoughts that the intent of evil might not connect them? The answer is not to be found in the corrupted heart because it is not capable of deducing something inconsistent with its nature—depraved—as Job declared: "Who can bring a clean thing out of an unclean?"[40] Although, one "would scarce imagine such an inward nest of wickedness;" says Charnock, "but God has affirmed it; and if any man should deny it, his own heart would give him the lie."[41]

---

38 Venema, *But for the Grace of God*, 141. There is a striking resemblance of this language found in Heidelberg Catechism Q&A 8: "But are we so corrupt that we are totally unable to do any good and inclined to all evil? Yes, unless we are regenerated by the Spirit of God." The Heidelberg Catechism makes it very clear that man is incapable of "doing any good."

39. Gen 6:5. NKJV.

40. Job 14:4 NKJV.

41. Charnock, "The Sinfulness and Cure of Thoughts," in *Works*, 5:17.

God brings man face-to-face with his wicked reality, especially when we consider the descriptors that are assigned (in Gen 6:5) to man's state of existence as a fallen creature—the magnitude: "wickedness was great"; the extent: "every intent of the thoughts"; the consistency: "only evil . . . continually." The words of Jer 17:9 further support this perspective when he proclaimed that "The heart is deceitful above all things, and desperately wicked; who can know it?"[42] Once again, we are faced with this absolute and universal terminology that seems to leave no room for anything other than the "totality" of the thoughts of the heart. The apostle Paul declares this same absolute universal truth in Eph 2:1, when he states that we "were dead in trespasses and sins."[43] Now it is clear, one is either dead or alive because you cannot exist in both states: "I am dead and alive." The law of non-contradiction, *principium contradictionis*, will not allow for such foolish logic. For example, I cannot say that "I am dead, and I am not dead" at the same time because the two terms are mutually exclusive; it is not possible for "A is B" and "A is not B" to be correct at the same time. That is, if you are dead, then the characteristic of your existence is defined by deadness and nothing else.[44] Man, the crown of creation, the beauty of God's image, was defaced, distorted, twisted, and deformed in his mind, heart, will, and

---

42 Jer 17:9. NKJV.

43. Eph 2:1. NKJV.

44 There needs to be a consideration of the Logic of Totality or the Logic of Depravity. What are the implications of this logic? For example, what is the purpose of depravity and the totality of it? From what point of view are we to consider the nature of this "total depravity"? Are there any assumptions about total depravity that we are making? What information do we have about total depravity and is it consistent with our understanding of it? Are there limitations to that information or our understanding? What are the implications of this total depravity from our understanding? What inferences can we make about total depravity that will help our understanding of it? What concepts or terms need to be identified and defined for us to approach total depravity properly? What questions surface in consideration of "total depravity" and our understanding of it? There needs to be an understanding of the language employed and to what extent the absoluteness applies to terminology. That is, can we have an absolute with limitations? If so, what does an absolute look like that has limitations? What limitations can you possibly have if something is identified as absolute? It would seem that the two thoughts are contrary. It would appear, as we work through this, that these latter questions are most applicable to the Canons' approach to defining the concept of "total depravity" and our understanding of it. Furthermore, we have two constructed systems (or two levels of reality) that provide content to this concept; that is, the totality of total in the finite temporal sense of understanding and the totality of total in the eternal, infinite sense of understanding. So, there is a necessity of perspective of limitations in a proper understanding of total depravity. Can something be "total" that is not "total"?

emotions and bent on his own destruction. Such a description of reality conveys the universality of this contrariety. For Charnock, it demonstrates the infinite distance from the imitable perfections of God's holiness. "By sin . . ." says Charnock, "man was left many leagues behind any resemblance to God . . . an infinite distance from any imitation of God's holiness, or any appearance before him in a garb of nature pleasing to him."[45]

The kernel, "totality," of depravity really does take root in the deep dark recesses of man's most inner being and from there springs forth into every aspect of his nature, (i.e., mind, heart, will, emotions). In other words, man has a natural predisposition in his "totality" (mind, heart, will, emotions). We could call this predisposition a *diathesis*, which is from the same Ancient Greek word, *diathesis* ("state, condition"), also *diatithenai* ("to arrange"). *Diathesis* is defined as a natural predisposition toward a particular state or condition and especially one that is abnormal or diseased.[46] So, it could be said that man's diathetical foundation is to be found (positioned) in the heart[47] of man, which could properly be identified as the epicenter of man from where everything is ushering forth. That is, man, in his fallen state, stripped of his extrinsic image of God,[48] which resulted in the natural elements of the soul (intellect, will, affections) being enshrouded in unrighteousness.

The outworking of this natural predisposition of "total depravity" rises from the internal kernel of sin, infiltrates all aspects of the faculties and manifests itself in the form of man "rebelling against God,"[49] which is

---

45   Charnock, "A Discourse upon the Holiness of God," in *Works*, 2:250.

46   "diathesis." *The American Heritage® Medical Dictionary.*

47   The term "heart," signifying that prevailing moral disposition that determines the volitions and actions, is the phrase most commonly used in Scripture—e.g., Matt 12:33, 35; 15:19; Luke 6:43, 45.

48   Turretin, *Institutes of Elenctic Theology*. Turretin distinguishes the image of God by the intrinsic and extrinsic. The former he assigns the intellect, will, and affections; the latter he assigns righteousness, holiness, and purity. Richard Muller makes the following distinction: "imago substantiatis" and "imago accidentalis." See Muller, A. *Dictionary of Latin and Greek Theological Terms*, 143–45.

49   *Canons of Dort* 1619, Chapter 1, Article 1. There should be some thought given to the inception of or the height of total depravity and its relation to "rebelling against God." That is, is the totality of depravity encapsulated within the rebellion or is rebellion the height of the totality of depravity? For example, is it possible to make such distinctions in one act being more depraved than another? If so, how does one make that distinction in the act? Alternatively, perhaps, the object of the act is the ultimate consideration of the degree of the depravity of the act.

considered to be the actual undercurrent that drives this hostility toward God.[50] Although there are proper distinctions to be made with the faculties of the soul, there is not one aspect of the faculties that resides outside of this unrighteous enshrouding, and to suggest otherwise only solidifies the truth of man's depraved state, because the "world understood not," says Charnock, "the extent of sin . . . sin of their nature . . . sin of unbelief."[51] For example, the intellect is not compartmentalized or segregated from this realm of depravity in such a way that it is protected from this depravity—it does not reside in a protected environment that is excluded. Rather, the strength of sin lies universally[52] in the faculties. That is, sin is universal in its decay of the faculties:[53] understanding, will, and affections, and so, our end to glorify God finds no answer in man's heart; instead, the heart has been made unfit to answer the end to glorify God. Once again this further demonstrates that "there is a necessity," says Charnock, "[that] he should be made over again, and created upon a better foundation, that some principle should be in him to oppose this universal depravation, enlighten his understanding, mollify his heart, and reduce his affections to their due order and object."[54] This is what is realized by the "new birth" or regeneration.

iii. Anatomy of Contrariety

Aristotle, in his book *The Metaphysics*,[55] writes about theory of potentiality and actuality. This concept of potentiality and actuality can be employed, to a degree, to help flesh out the aspect of "totality" in depravity, more specifically, the perspective of depravity.

However, even with this we still fall short of the "totality" in the depravity of man. According to Aristotle, this potentiality is nothing at all, at least, it is nothing until it is actualized. That is, if A possesses the potential to

---

50. Vos, *Reformed Dogmatics*, 2:58. cf. "Total depravity . . . does mean that by nature no love for God is present as the motivating principle of our life: that it does not dwell in us as a disposition and therefore never determines our deeds, thoughts, and words; and, conversely, that in our entire life there is an undertow of hostility toward God that only needs an external stimulus to develop into conscious opposition toward the Lord. There is no spiritual good in us."

51. Charnock, "A Discourse of Conviction of Sin," in *Works*, 4:169.
52. Charnock, "A Discourse of the Nature of Regeneration," in *Works*, 3:146.
53. Charnock, "The Necessity of Regeneration," in *Works*, 3:17.
54. Charnock, "The Necessity of Regeneration," in *Works*, 3:17.
55. Aristotle, *The Metaphysics*, 1028b–11041b.

be A, its potentiality to be A is reduced as it is actualized and becomes A. The result, is that we need to introduce some concept of degrees into the discussion of "totality," because the totality of man's depravity does not reside in a vacuous realm, nor is it "nothingness." Instead, it is a real aspect of man's natural make-up and is the epicenter of his heart. However, the potentiality and actuality run on two parallel levels (spiritual intentionality and human act), that is, the potentiality has become an actuality in the nature of man's soul (i.e., faculties, intellect, will, and heart); he is dead from the totality of sin. Furthermore, the potentiality and actuality of acting this out are thwarted, to an extent, because on the surface (human actions), we see, perhaps, a closer alignment with the previous example. Therefore, if A possesses the potential to be A—man not only possess the capacity of sin; indeed, sin possesses man—then its potentiality to be A is reduced as it is actualized and becomes A. Consequently, the latter part is something that we humans only see glimpses of in the world around us in the heinous acts of man's depravity. At the same time, there is an aspect of discontinuity in this reality which is significant because the discontinuity is a limited understanding of reality, especially if the grace of God is not factored into the equation because we see attributes of depravity, as well as glimpses of kindness, love, patience, etc., which is nothing short of God's grace. The grace of God should not be confused as the goodness of man's heart; rather, it would be better identified as man's simple act of self-preservation.[56]

Interesting enough, there is a sense of a rational/irrational aspect in Aristotle's potentiality. That is, there can be a rational potentiality to produce medication for the sick, however, as has been seen it can make one healthier or make one sicker. There is also the irrational potentiality of water that can only make things wet and not dry. Aristotle did speak to the rational/irrational aspect of potentiality; that is, in the sense of the agent of

---

56. Boettner, *The Reformed Doctrine of Predestination*, 61. Boettner provides a bit of insight into the extant of this depravity, he states, "This doctrine of Total Inability, which declares that men are dead in sin, does not mean that all men are equally bad, nor that any man is as bad as he could be, nor that any one is entirely destitute of virtue, nor that human nature is evil in itself, nor that man's spirit is inactive, and much less does it mean that the body is dead. What it does mean is that since the fall man rests under the curse of sin, that he is *actuated by wrong principles*, and that he is wholly unable to love God or to do anything meriting salvation. His corruption is *extensive* but not necessarily *intensive*" [emphasis mine]. There is a significant portion of content rolled into this concept of "self-preservation" and has an impact on our understanding of depravity. Once again, it is necessary to understand the nature of this depravity in light of what Scripture says about man's spiritual state.

change being rational or something that unfolds naturally. This rational/irrational analogy closely treads along the deep-rooted path of sin that is pervasive in the heart of man. Irrationality is deep-seated within the depth of man's depraved heart, and it is known as unbelief, which manifests itself in rebellion against the Creator. Hence, Charnock concludes: "*causa causae est causa causati*, may be justly charged upon our score."[57]

It is essential that we account for the substratum of this potentiality and actuality within the context of "total depravity." The predisposition of man that is rooted in his natural makeup provides the substratum, to a certain extent, the environment for the potentiality and actuality when considering man in his depraved state. This predisposition of man is the very thing that the *Canons of Dort* identify in Article 1—3. For example, the image of God has been just short of annihilated;[58] the mind has been significantly impacted by sin—that is, the noetic effect of sin ("blindness, terrible darkness, futility, and distortion of judgment in his mind"[59]), the will, and heart have been diverted by "perversity, defiance, and hardness,"[60] and the emotions have become the wellspring for lust ("impurity in all his emotions"[61]). So, in this sense, the potentiality of man's "total depravity" has, indeed, become an actuality.

Moreover, in this sense, man is, indeed, in the very most inner recesses of his soul "totally" depraved,[62] and from there emanations of that

---

57. Charnock, "The Sinfulness and Cure of Thoughts," in *Works*, 5:24. According to Nichols's translation, "The cause of a cause is also the cause of that which is subsequently caused."

58. Calvin speaks of the decimation of the image of God; however, he notes that there is a remnant, a spark that does remain within man. However, it should be pointed out that some believe that the "image of God" has been completely destroyed and does not remain. If so, how do we deal with Gen 9:6 still referring to a man as being in the "image of God." Feenstra, *Unspeakable Comfort: A Commentary on the Canons of Dort*, 104–5. Feenstra suggests that this is the Canons position. He notes, "Through rebellion and disobedience mankind is no longer God's representative. The remains of the image of God are no longer stamped upon him. As the following articles [2–5] will demonstrate, the Lord has to make an entirely new beginning with us." If this is the position of the Canons, then where does this "light of nature" come from that the Canons reference?

59. *Canons* of Dort 1619, Chapter 1, Article 1.

60 *Canons* of Dort 1619, Chapter 1, Article 1.

61 *Canons* of Dort 1619, Chapter 1, Article 1.

62 It could be said that at this level of dealing with man (inner recesses of his soul) that both the potentiality and the actuality are recognized in the totality. The words of the Canons, Article 3, "inclined to evil, dead in their sins, and slaves to sin . . . they are neither willing nor able to return to God." His natural potentiality is derived from his

depravity bubble to the surface. However, the potentiality of the depths of that depravity does not come to full actuality, because the depravity that is emanated from the depravity of man is sifted, stunted, and constrained by the grace of God. Charnock illustrates the depths of depravity in reference to the substance of an act.

Although, we are aware, to some extent, the "total" potentiality of that depravity, the Creator only knows the "totality" of the actuality of depravity. That is, the "least speck and atom of dust in every chink of this little world," says Charnock, "is known and censured by God."[63] Paul gives a more vivid picture of what God sees when the fallen man is considered outside of Christ; he declares the full reality of man's spiritual death:

> Being filled with all unrighteousness, wickedness, greed, evil; full of envy, murder, strife, deceit, malice; they are gossips, slanderers, haters of God, insolent, arrogant, boastful, inventors of evil, disobedient to parents, without understanding, untrustworthy, unloving, unmerciful: Who knowing the judgement of God, that they which commit such things are worthy of death, not only do the same, but have pleasure in them that do them. Rom. 1:29–32

The depravity is comprehensive, and this applies to the various faculties that are housed within the soul of man; this is the panoramic view that the Creator has of his creatures, and these are the parts and the sum of those parts in its totality. This panoramic perspective is the "totality" of the "total" in the depravity of man, and from God's perspective it is not only total, but it is unqualified and undiminished, it is absolute. The extensiveness of the Creator's panoramic view is described by Charnock as follows: "God hath taken an exact survey of the whole world in its dark and fallen state" in its totality. The Creator upon his survey of this iniquitous existence of man "could not, among those multitudes of acts which spring from the will of man," Charnock notes, "find one piece of beauty, one particle of the divine image, for he hath pronounced this sentence upon them, with repetition, too, as his infallible judgment. 'There is none righteous, no, not one: they

---

natural state of depravity, which inherently defines what his actuality will be . . . "inclined to evil" because he is "dead" and bound to his depravity. Furthermore, the "total depravity" also defines our capacity to make the slightest movement toward God. As noted, by Rev. deCock, when he spoke before Secession of 1834 in the Netherlands: "If I had to add even one sigh to my salvation, I would be forever lost." The source of this quote is from *Notes on the Canons of Dort*.

63. Charnock, "A Discourse of the Sinfulness and Cure of Thoughts," in *Works*, 5:297.

are all gone out of the way, they are together become unprofitable; there is none that doeth good, no, not one,' Rom 3:10–12."[64]

That is what God sees in the actual fallen man and the iniquitous reality of his existence outside of Christ. It was this very reality that the framers of the *Canons* sought to convey from the Scriptures in response to the Remonstrants who sought to offer a doctrine of regeneration that was somehow framed around the potentiality of man, as opposed to the actuality of man's depravity before a holy Creator. It was this very structure that the men of that period, known as High Orthodoxy, sought to fill with additional scriptural content in the exposition of Scripture.

We find Charnock expounding upon the reality of man's spiritually dead existence as a defining characteristic of the soul outside of Christ, and this is vividly depicted in Charnock's *Discourse on the Sinfulness and Cure of Thoughts*. This particular discourse is an exposition of the Gen 6:5, and the continuity of this discourse with the doctrine set forth by the *Canons of Dort* are undeniable. The purpose in setting forth the position of the *Canons of Dort* is twofold: first, to further illustrate what Mueller identified with this period leading up to High Orthodoxy; that is, the construction of the doctrinal skeleton that high orthodoxy would further develop. Second, to demonstrate that Charnock, indeed, did further develop and fill in the skeleton with the scriptural understanding of man's depravity, which established the foundation for the necessity of redemption to be found in Christ alone. It is with the description mentioned above of the spiritual reality of man that we are confronted with the exceptional degree of beauty that has been defaced, and the beauty of that conformity to holiness has been changed into deformity. So it is with this understanding that we see how "dreadfully are we fallen," declares Charnock, "not only to lame ourselves, but dead ourselves, that we cannot rise again, as a man fallen may!" This strong language of Charnock, "lame ourselves" and "dead ourselves," is expressed elsewhere—"unman themselves"[65]—and it is an attempt to expose the core of our existence outside of Christ, not to mention the fact that as a result of this success to "dead ourselves" we have become "so unconceivably

---

64. Charnock, "A Discourse of the Efficient of Regeneration," in *Works*, 3:180.

65. Charnock, "The Chief Sinners Objects of Choicest Mercy," in *Works*, 5:534. He notes, "God lets men run on so far in sin, that they do unman themselves, that he may proclaim to all the world that we are unable to do anything of ourselves at first towards our recovery without a superior principle."

changed from what we were, that we cannot be recovered without a new make, without a new birth."[66]

It is, therefore, in light of man's active efforts to be in a continual state of lameness and deadness that our expectation of mankind in their depraved states is that they will "row against the stream of [their] own conscience,"[67] and will continually and voluntarily submit themselves as "slave[s] to their own lusts, which they serve with as delightful, as disgraceful, a drudgery against the light of their own minds."[68] It is from this that Charnock concludes that the principle of contrariety to God is seated within mankind's very nature and manifests itself in the most egregious ways before the face of God, all the while turning a deaf ear to the Creator's voice and "their ears open to the least whisper of Satan."[69] It is this deeply implanted principle of contrariety that manifests itself in the totality of man. It is from this contrariety to or aversion to God which "proceeds our stupidity, the folly of our thoughts, the levity of our minds, the deadness of our affections, the sleepiness of our souls, our inexcusable carelessness in holy duties, more than anything of a temporal concern, but from this aversion from God!"[70] Moreover, this "aversion from God" is nothing less than an aversion to his holiness or as Charnock explains it:

> [God] did not take angels for his pattern in the first polishing the soul, but himself. In defacing this image, we cast dirt upon the holiness of God, which was his pattern in the framing of us, and rather choose to be conformed to Satan, who is God's grand enemy, to have God's image wiped out of us, and the devil's pictured in us.[71]

So it is, with Charnock's scriptural understanding of the nature, scope, and effect of the totality of man's depravity which has manifested itself in the principle of contrariety. This principle of contrariety allows him to situate his doctrine of regeneration, which must be found in the Scriptures as well; hence, we now get a better picture of the necessity of regeneration. The reality of contrariety between the Creator and the creature will not, by any shape of the imagination, allow for the principle of contrariety to be supplanted by a principle of holiness without a change in man's fallen

---

66 Charnock, "The Necessity of Regeneration," in *Works*, 3:58.
67. Charnock, "Man's Enmity to God," in *Works*, 5:515.
68. Charnock, "Man's Enmity to God," in *Works*, 5:515.
69. Charnock, "Man's Enmity to God," in *Works*, 5:515.
70. Charnock, "Man's Enmity to God," in *Works*, 5:515.
71. Charnock, "A Discourse upon the Holiness of God," in *Works*, 2:243.

nature. Man is in no position to offer up a solution to his deadly predicament; there is nothing he can possibly offer up in the way of reconciling the contrarieties that now define his existence. "The old frame must be demolished," Charnock says, "and a new one reared, for a change of state cannot be without a change of nature. It is impossible that this nature, so corrupt and contrary, can ever be reconciled to the pure and holy nature of God; what communion hath light with darkness?"[72]

The principle of contrariety brings us back to the fundamental issue with approaching a doctrine of regeneration. There must be an accurate identification of the problem that a real solution might be offered up to fix the actual problem, not a pretended constructed problem that has failed to account for the reality. Therefore, because "there was an universal depravation by the fall," Charnock says, "regeneration must answer it in its extensiveness in every faculty. Otherwise it is not the birth of the man, but of one part only. It is but a new piece, not a new creature. This or that faculty may be said to be new, not the soul, not the man."[73]

---

72. Charnock, "Man's Enmity to God," in *Works*, 5:515.
73 Charnock, "The Necessity of Regeneration," in *Works*, 3:27.

IV

Re-tethering the Strands of Conformity

IT STANDS TO REASON that if man's natural state is defined by the totality of its corruption, its depravity, then to change that natural state of depravity would require something just as extensive. So, in speaking about the totality aspect of depravity, it would intrinsically require us to speak to the necessity of regeneration[1] that would change the totality of that corruption.

---

1. There is not enough space in this work to go into detail of all those who wrote on this topic of regeneration; however, it is crucial to give a glimpse of some of the men who wrote about this subject, because it gives us a sense of the importance of the doctrine of regeneration during this time period. Also, the amount of material on this subject demonstrated that there was a concerted effort to construct a system that was coherent with the truth of Scripture, i.e., God's sovereignty, man's responsibility, and the condition of man in his depraved state. This truth is evident in the writings of the following men: Franciscus Junius (1545-1642), I have included Junius because of the significant role he played in the development of a Calvinist concept of the will. Gomarus, *Disputatio theologica de libero arbitrio*. I have included Gomarus because of the significant role he played in the development of the Canons of Dort 1619. Sibbes, *The Complete Works of Richard Sibbes*, 7:127-28. 'The Touchstone of Regeneration' forms No. 24 of 'The Saint's Cordials' of 1629. Whatley, *The New Birth: Or, a Treatise of Regeneration*. Dickson, *Therepeutica sacra* shewing briefly the method of healing the diseases of the conscience, concerning regeneration. Maccovius, *Disputatio Theologica De Regeneratione*. Burgess, *Spiritual Refining A Treatise of Grace and Assurance*. Thomas Goodwin (1600-1680), Isaac Ambrose (1604-1664), Thomas Manton (1620-1677), William Bates (1625-1699), Grebenitz, *Tractatus theologicus de regenertione, trinbus disputationibus*. Cole, *A Discourse of Regeneration*. 124 pages devoted to the subject of regeneration. Hopkins, "The Nature and Necessity of Regeneration," in *The Works of Ezekiel Hopkins*, vol. 2. There are 80 pages devoted to the subject of regeneration. Swinnock, *The Door of Salvation Opened by the Key of Regeneration*, vol. 5. 260 pages devoted to the subject of regeneration. Peter Van Mastricht (1630-1706), Mastricht, *A Treatise on Regeneration*. 63 pages

"Regeneration of the soul," says Charnock, "is of absolute necessity to a gospel and glorious state."[2]

In *Man's Fourfold State*, Thomas Boston points to the correlation that exists between the corrupt state of man and the necessity of that divine work to change the corrupt state of man. "The corruption of our nature," Boston says, "shews the absolute necessity of regeneration." The correlative relation is implied within the corrupted state of man, which would necessitate the necessity of regeneration to deal with that corruption. That is, according to Boston, "the absolute necessity of regeneration plainly proves the corruption of our nature; for why should a man need a second birth, if his nature were not quite marred in his first birth?"[3] Swinnock follows this to its logical conclusion, "Yet it is a thing of absolute necessity and therefore,"[4] Swinnock concludes, "must not be neglected."[5] The employment of the definitive language, "absolute necessity," is intentional and it has in mind the true or real state of man's condition or his current existence—he is dead—outside of Christ. So, it "is not a work of indifferency, which may be done or may not be done," Swinnock says, "but a work of indispensable necessity, which must be done, or thou art undone for ever."[6]

This "absolute necessity" of regeneration is a reality that Charnock would explore in a number of discourses. More specifically, those on the doctrine of regeneration,[7] and he would do so comprehensively and

---

devoted to the subject of regeneration. Clarkson, "The New Creature," in *The Works of David Clarkson*, 2:9. Charnock, *The Works of Stephen Charnock*, vol. 3. 338 pages devoted to the subject of regeneration. Strimesius, *Tractatus theologicus de regeneratione, tribus disputationibus*.

2 Charnock, "The Necessity of Regeneration," in *Works*, 3:15.

3. Boston, *The Whole Works of Thomas Boston: Human Nature in Its Fourfold State*, 8:32. It should be noted that Boston's declaration of the "absolute necessity of regeneration" was not mere fodder to fill up space in his sermon; instead, it was an absolute reality for him. Consider the following in his address to his children. "See the absolute necessity of regeneration, the change of your nature, by union with Jesus Christ the second Adam; as it was corrupted by means of your relation to the first Adam fallen. Labour for the experience of the power of religion in your own souls, that you may have an argument for the reality of it, from your spiritual sense and feeling; and cleave to the Lord, his way of holiness." See Boston, *The Whole Works of Thomas Boston*, 12: vii.

4 Swinnock, *The Works of George Swinnock*, 5:188.

5 Swinnock, *The Works of George Swinnock*, 5:188.

6 Swinnock, *The Works of George Swinnock*, 5:188.

7. Volume 3 contains the following: *The Necessity of Regeneration; A Discourse of the Nature of Regeneration; A Discourse of the Efficient of Regeneration; A Discourse of the Word, the Instrument of Regeneration; A Discourse of God's Being the Author of*

emphatically. It is in this emphatic manner that we see Charnock revealing his soul's conviction about the necessity of regeneration, and this can be seen throughout his discourses where he continually marks off the necessity by emphatic descriptors. For example, in speaking of the nature of change brought about in regeneration it is not just a "change"; rather a "real change of the subject,"[8] "a real and mighty change wrought in him."[9] Operations in the soul are real; there is "real power to act . . . a real habit as the spring of them . . . real spiritual actions.[10] In each case, these descriptors would serve to further demonstrate the element of necessity, "absolute necessity" of the work of regeneration. Therefore, "this necessity," Charnock says, "is not founded only in the command of God that we should be renewed, but in the very nature of the thing, because God, in regard of his holiness, cannot converse with an impure creature."[11] It is here, in the words "because God, in regard of his holiness" that Charnock delineates and brings into focus the entirety of the situation. This center of reality, "in regard of his holiness" which directs the absolute necessity of regeneration that must supplant the defining principle of contrariety with a principle of conformity. "Can this be any otherwise done," asks Owen, "but by holiness of heart and life, by conformity to God in our souls, and living unto God in fruitful obedience?"[12]

Reconciliation; and *A Discourse of the Cleansing Virtue of Christ's Blood*. A.T.B. McGowen, in his dissertation on Thomas Boston, uses Charnock's doctrine of regeneration format as the basis of his chapter dealing with Thomas Boston's doctrine of regeneration. As McGowen points out, "We make substantial use of Stephen Charnock's classic volume on regeneration, which is arguably the best available text on the subject from a Reformed perspective." Also, McGowen notes the familiarity of Boston with Charnock's work on regeneration, and he says, "A reading of Boston on regeneration suggests that he was familiar with the work of this great Puritan writer, especially given the use he makes of certain arguments and expressions." See McGowen, "The Federal Theology of Thomas Boston," 169. I would suggest that there is a more significant influence on Boston than just Charnock's doctrine of regeneration, as will be noted elsewhere in this thesis, Boston uses large sections of Charnock's words in different areas of his works.

8. Charnock, "The Necessity of Regeneration," in *Works*, 3:15.
9. Charnock, "A Discourse of the Nature of Regeneration," in *Works*, 3:86.
10. Charnock, "A Discourse of the Nature of Regeneration," in *Works*, 3:94.
11. Charnock, "The Necessity of Regeneration," in *Works*, 3:23. This is seen in the wilderness wonderings, especially at Mt. Sinai. See Exod 20.
12. Owen, *The Works of John Owen*, 3:649.

a. The Necessity of Continuity in Conformity

It would seem contraposition to suggest that something is being brought into conformity of something (i.e., Redeemer-redeemed, God's holiness), yet, that conformity is characterized by discontinuity; instead of conformity. This anomaly would seem to beg the question, can discontinuity be the basis for conformity? If that is the case, how are we to speak about conformity which is inherently defined, to an extent, by a reality of continuity? The relationship of continuity and discontinuity as it pertains to the conformity of a soul to God's imitable perfections are of central importance for Charnock, especially as it pertains to the realm of regeneration. "No house can possibly be built without a foundation; the groundwork first, then the superstructure."[13]

The lack of consideration of either has caused many to be led astray by some apparitional form of regeneration instead of the reality of regeneration, which relates directly back to having the real problem in view in order to identify the real solution (i.e., the depravity of man). Although, some would associate this issue with the modern movement within the church at the time, that was not the actual circumstances. Instead, we find that men of this epoch were on guard against this discontinuity of regenerational conformity to Christ, and proclaiming, clearly, the aspect of continuity that always should be a defining characteristic of the reality of regeneration, which is not only a soul's conformity to the Creator but also the soul's conformity to its Redeemer.[14]

Consequently, when Charnock speaks of the reality of regeneration, he does so emphatically—the "real" real is real grace, real holiness, etc. Charnock was not alone in his insistent language about the reality of regeneration. For example, John Owen was just as insistent about the issue of continuity and discontinuity in regeneration when he discussed that differences between "reformation" and "renovation" in the life of one who has been exposed to transforming work of the Spirit of God.

---

13. Charnock, "The Knowledge of God," in *Works*, 4:70.

14. Charnock, "A Discourse of Self-Examination," in *Works*, 4:493. Charnock notes that we who stand in a Redeemer-redeemed relationship should "see what workmanship of God there is in our souls, and what conformity there is between us and our Creator, between us and Redeemer." Although this phrase is in Charnock's *A Discourse of Self-Examination*, which is his sermon on 2 Cor 13:5, it does speak to another aspect of conformity, that of intimacy in that conformity; that is, union with God through Christ the Redeemer.

Among various Puritans, this continuity is identified as an actual regenerative act brought about by the work of the Spirit and not just a "moral reformation."[15] This continuity was identified as not being a partial reality that seemed to have its foot partially in a new life and partially in the old life for periods of time. Also, this speaks to the fact that it is not just a "reformation" of life. Rather, a "renovation" of life, although not necessarily the distinction on the words; nonetheless, this was something that the Puritans stressed. John Owen, for example, notes that "regeneration doth not consist in a moral reformation of life and conversation"[16]; rather, it is the "whole nature" that is subject to God's work of real holiness, which is communicated to all parts of the soul, not just within a particular faculty. "This did not consist in reformation of life," says Owen, "no, nor in a course of virtuous actions." And from this Owen notes the reason, because man "was created in the image of God before he had done any one good thing at all, or was capable of so doing."[17] This image of God is extensive and principally defined by "uprightness, rectitude, and ability of his whole soul, his mind, will, and affections, in, unto, and for the obedience that God required of him."[18] This extensive work of the Spirit is echoed by Charnock, as well. "It is a universal change of the whole man," says Charnock, which means that it is "a new creature" and with the new creature there is "a new power or new faculty." This newness "extends to every part; understanding, will, conscience, affections, all were corrupted by sin, all are renewed by grace."[19]

15. Boston outlines what could be associated with this "moral reformation," however, should not be confused with holiness. Boston identifies three things: First, "common civility," where a man may conduct himself in a civil, courthouse, discreet manner, "yet be a stranger to holiness." Second, "morality" in the sense of honesty or conformity to the law, yet lacking in relationship to Christ and his Spirit. Lastly, "form" of godliness which pertains to external duties of religion, yet no real holiness. See Boston, "The Mystery of Sanctification by Christ," in *Works,* 6:615.

16 Owen, *Discourse Concerning the Holy Spirit,* 3:217, he notes, "We say and believe that regeneration consists in spirituali renovatione naturae,– "in a spiritual renovation of our nature"; our modern Socinians, that it doth so in morali reformatione vitae, "in a moral reformation of life."

17. Owen, *The Works of John Owen,* 3:222.

18. Owen, *The Works of John Owen,* 3:222.

19. Charnock, "A Discourse of the Nature of Regeneration," *The Complete in Works,* 3:95. See Reuter, "William Ames: The Leading Theologian in the Awakening of Reformed Pietism," in *William Ames,* 191–5. "Apart from the will, the emotions have no real home, according to him, but live rather within it, be they good or bad, and give the will corresponding activity. Ames feels the kinship between feeling and will to be so close at their deepest point that they are at times for him interchangeable terms." See Sibbes,

The notion that no partial or disjunctive character is a part of the new creation in a scriptural regeneration was expressed by Oliver Heywood (1630–1702) expressed this reality when he stated that a "partial reformation is no sound evidence of regeneration: the unclean spirit of scandalous sinning may go out of the devil's slave for a season."[20] Matthew Mead draws a potent distinction, and he suggests that there is a deceitful element to this act of "reformation" that man attempts to heighten his ability toward expelling the "corrupt habits from the will, and reduce it to the true object."[21] That is, "some are deceived with a half work, taking conviction for conversion, reformation for regeneration."[22] This reducing to its true object is what Charnock directly connects to the supernatural function of grace, and the conformity induces a continuity to that conformity. Therefore, a "supernatural renewing grace," says Charnock, "must expel corrupt habits from the will, and reduce it to its true object."[23]

According to Owen, there is no shortage of those who have are perishing under the sin of apostasy or hypocrisy. Rather, "it is the case of thousands in the world" because the failure identifies the evangelical sense of the work of regeneration in the soul of man. As a result of the "evangelical sense," there is a division between real holiness and not-real holiness. There is an "inward purity and real holiness: when some are said to be holy, and that also two ways," says Owen, "for either they are so really and in the truth of the thing itself, or in estimation only, and that either of themselves or others."[24] Although, this distinctive reality of holiness exists, nonetheless, there are many who "have account[ed] themselves to be holy, and been pure in their own eyes." However, they are lacking that necessary component that draws the line of reality between "moral reformation" and "regeneration"; they "were never washed from their iniquity."[25]

The Complete Works of Richard Sibbes, 2:46. "The word heart, you know, includes the whole soul, for the understanding is the heart, 'an understanding heart,' Job 38:36. To ' lay things up in our hearts,' Luke 2:51, there it is memory; and to cleave in heart is to cleave in will, Acts 11:23. To 'rejoice in heart,' Isa. 30:29, that is in the affection. So that all the powers of the soul, the inward man, as Paul calleth it, 2 Cor. 4:16, is the heart."

20. Heywood, *The Whole Works of the Rev. Oliver Heywood*, 5:77.
21. Charnock, *The Doctrine of Regeneration*, 303.
22 Mead, *The Almost Christian Discovered*, 180–81.
23. Charnock, "The Necessity of Regeneration," in *Works*, 3:34.
24. Owen, *The Works of John Owen*, 11:89.
25. Owen, *The Works of John Owen*, 11:222.

In lockstep fashion with these men it is noted that an "[o]utward reformation is not sufficient," Charnock says, because "[r]egeneration is never without reformation of life."[26] Not to mention that one's profession "may be false, outward reformation may be but as a painted sepulchre."[27] The distinction between "reformation of life" and "regeneration" is an essential line in the sand that not only should be drawn, but also one that should be adhered to because there must be continuity in the coming to life within the regenerative act of the Word and Spirit. If not, we find ourselves dealing with Scripture that has been compromised or Scripture that is not able to speak full truths. In addition, what becomes of the new life, hope, eternal life, and any other aspect of redemption when this one thread is unraveling. Hence, the emphasis on the "reality" or the "new creation" because the man who has been made new will not be driven about by the principles that once defined his nature; his *diathesis* has been remolded or recast into a new form. This new creation is and should continue to be a significant aspect of defining the parameters of our understanding of God's work, especially within the confines of Scripture. Even here, we have Charnock guarding against the slightest consideration that man may have something to do with the transformation from death to life. Furthermore, this points to the inseparable reality and continuity to be found within the natural makeup of man before and after regeneration.

Therefore, as Charnock states, "Outward reformation is not sufficient" because it is nothing more than a form without the substance; a mere mirage of something that cannot possibly be real, because "[r]egeneration is never without reformation of life."[28] This reality, for Charnock, is a further manifestation of the corruption of the heart in its attempt to cover-up and deceive itself. Nonetheless, the two are inseparable, and there must be continuity in the reality that resides within the depths of man's soul when the Spirit works a new life and the outward life. In some sense, it does not matter which terms we want to employ—whether it is "reformation" or "renovation" because what matters is the content and substance of either word used. So, if it is "reformation" or "renovation" in the life of a person—if it is only on the surface—there will be no continuity in the outward reflection of the inward reality; rather, a reality that is skewed with no real basis for its existence, a facade.

26. Charnock, "The Necessity of Regeneration," in *Works*, 3:59–60.
27 Charnock, "The Necessity of Regeneration," in *Works*, 3:93.
28. Charnock, "The Necessity of Regeneration," in *Works*, 3:59–60.

Furthermore, if there is no outward reflection of the inward reality, then the inward reality becomes a subject of scrutiny and a question of what is real within the soul of man. Any attempt to suggest otherwise speaks to the depths of foolishness to be found in the mind of a depraved man. Charnock speaks to this reality when he notes: "Though a natural heart hath some broken pieces of the law of God deposited in it, yet *there is not the least syllable of Christ or regeneration writ in the mind by the hand of nature.*"[29]

If there "is not the least syllable of Christ or regeneration writ in the mind by the hand of nature," where is it that man thinks he might locate the reality of holiness or potential for good? Is it to be identified in his will? If so, "how can he by his corrupt will recover that purity which he hath lost?"[30] Perhaps man is to find this source of good in his affections? However, such a source only seems to expose the principle of contrariety further, because "the interest of his corrupt affection excites him to a loathing of that which is truly good."[31] Maybe we need to look to the understanding of the innate capacity of good that man is looking to discover? Is it to be located in the understanding? If so, can the understanding properly prepare itself for the reception of the gospel?[32] Although, inherent within any idea we might identify a particular faculty that is somehow more enlightened than another and, therefore, that faculty might function as a source of good only to illustrate the discontinuity further. Does man find it amongst the "pieces of the law of God" that are deposited in his heart? What absurdity is associated with the notion that man, in sifting through the pieces of the law of God is going to find amongst the rubble clues to the capacity of goodness to be found in his fallen nature? Instead, what man will find in those "pieces of the law of God" is the reflection of a dead and dying soul that is utterly lost outside of Christ, and this is where he will see, perhaps, a semblance of congruity; that is, there is "an inveterate alienation of heart . . . in men from real holiness,"[33] observes William Bates.

---

29. Charnock, "A Discourse of the Efficient of Regeneration," in *Works*, 3:186.
30. Charnock, "A Discourse of the Efficient of Regeneration," in *Works*, 3:195.
31. Charnock, "Man's Enmity to God," in *Works*, 5:475.
32. Charnock, "A Discourse of the Efficient of Regeneration," in *Works*, 3:186.
33. Bates, *The Whole Works of the Rev. William Bates*, 3:479. Was this not the case, for example, with Paul? Consider Paul's reflection upon the law of God and its impact in Rom 7:7–14: "What shall we say then? Is the law sin? Certainly not! On the contrary, I would not have known sin except through the law. For I would not have known covetousness unless the law had said, "You shall not covet." But sin, taking opportunity by the

To offer up an alternate reality would require that we disown Christ and what is real, because what purpose would we have of Christ or regeneration if a man had some internal point of goodness that he could draw from to create himself anew. "The understanding therefore," concludes Charnock, "naturally cannot prepare itself for the reception of the gospel, because it hath not any principle in it which suits the doctrine of it."[34] It does not have this principle because there "is not true holiness," says Boston, "but in communion with Christ." Furthermore, Boston notes, "Men may have a shew and semblance of holiness, without union and communion with Christ. But real holiness acceptable to God, no man attains but in Christ, being sanctified only with his blood, by his Spirit, through faith; made new creatures after his image, by participation of the all-fulness of grace in him, as at large declared, 1 Cor. 1:2; Eph. 2:10; 1 Pet. 1:2; Acts 26:18."[35]

The inherent nature of conformity to God's imitable perfections is to be grounded in reality and not in some concocted notion of man, as if a particular faculty has some kernel of holiness that might rise to the surface when summoned by that faculty. That is incongruous with the state of a man outside of Christ. Furthermore, any attempt to define the boundaries of conformity to God's holiness that is not grounded, built upon, and structured with the grace of God amounts to nothing more than a moral reformation. However, the summation of this congruity—inherent in the new life found in the work of God through Christ—is identified by John Sheffield in his sermon, *Of Holiness*. "That true and real holiness," says Sheffield, "is the grace, the duty, the state, the trade which every Christian is bound to follow, pursue, press after with might and main, as he ever thinks to look God in the face."[36]

---

commandment, produced in me all manner of evil desire. For apart from the law sin was dead. I was alive once without the law, but when the commandment came, sin revived and I died. And the commandment, which was to bring life, I found to bring death. For sin, taking occasion by the commandment, deceived me, and by it killed me. Therefore the law is holy, and the commandment holy and just and good. Has then what is good become death to me? Certainly not! But sin, that it might appear sin, was producing death in me through what is good, so that sin through the commandment might become exceedingly sinful. For we know that the law is spiritual, but I am carnal, sold under sin."

34. Charnock, "A Discourse of the Efficient of Regeneration," in *Works*, 3:188.
35. Boston, "The Mystery of Sanctification by Christ," in *Works* 6:614–15.
36. Nichols, *Puritan Sermons*, 5:427.

b. Creational Conformity—Regeneration

There is coherence in the Puritans's thinking of the freedom of the will with those that went before them (e.g., Augustine and Calvin). This aspect of regeneration[37] and the free will of man was a hotbed for debate during their time, especially in the formation of the Belgic Confession and the Canons of Dort. It is fundamental to the Calvinist understanding of the scriptural teachings on regeneration.[38] Fransiscus Junius,[39] one who was tasked with making minor revisions to the Belgic Confession advocated

---

37 Van Til and Eric H. Sigward, *Unpublished Manuscripts of Cornelius Van Til*, 71. "In accordance with this detraction from Christ's actual and complete accomplishment of salvation for the sinner goes a changing about of the judicial and reformatory work of Christ in the hearts of men. All forms of nomistic soteriology give precedence to the reformatory work of Christ and make the judicial element secondary. This is a very serious error. Another indication of this form of soteriology is that as a rule it does not distinguish between those acts that take place within consciousness as e.g., faith, and those that take place below consciousness, e.g., regeneration. It conceives of all these acts as taking place within consciousness, for it is the will of man that ultimately decides and no room is left for an immediate subconscious working of the Spirit. Moreover it does not make regeneration the basis of the later reformatory acts but places all these acts on a par, and finally, it does not conceive of every part in the *ordo salutis* as being a putting away of the old man and a putting on of the new, but emphasizes chiefly the putting on of the new for the sinfulness of man is then not a very serious matter."

38. Owen, *Display of Arminianism*, 62–63. Owen speaks of the "effectual working of his, according to his eternal purpose, whereby though some agents as the wills of men are causes free and indefinite or unlimited, lords of their own actions." Furthermore, Owen continues, "in respect of their internal principle of operations (that is, their own nature), they are yet all, in respect of his decree, and by his powerful working, determined to this and that effect in particular; not that they are compelled to do this, or hindered from doing that, but are inclined and disposed to do this or that according to their proper manner of working, that is most freely . . . We grant as large a freedom and dominion to our wills over their own acts as a creature subject to the supreme rule of God's providence is capable of. Endued we are with such a liberty of will as is free from all outward compulsion and inward necessity, having an elective faculty of applying itself unto that which seems good unto it, in which it has a free choice, notwithstanding it is subservient to the decree of God . . . the acts of will being positive entities . . . cannot have their essence and existence solely from the will itself, and cannot be thus, auto on, a first and supreme cause endued with an underived being." He distinguishes between will "as it was at first by God created . . . and . . . will as it is now by sin corrupted; yet being considered in that estate also, they ascribe more unto it than it was ever capable of." *The Doctrine of the Saints' Perseverance Explained and Confirmed*. He says, "the impotency that is in us to do good is not amiss termed ethico-pysica, both natural and moral." These extracts give the views entertained by Puritans who meant to express the doctrines written on the very face of Scripture, but sometimes did so by doubtful metaphysical distinctions.

39. Van Asselt, *Reformed Thought of Freedom*, 121.

three different realities in order to make the distinction of man's nature and man's free potency and necessity, which, "arises from man's own nature and not from any factor from outside." Accordingly, Junius derived "three states after the fall,"[40] alternatively, realities which demonstrate the "distinctive marks of each reality is the relation of man to the good and to the bad."[41] In other words, man has a natural predisposition, and here, Charnock, echoing these sentiments, states that "there is no object proposed to man, but his active nature may, *according to the goodness or badness of his disposition*, make good or an ill use of" [emphasis mine].[42] Hence, the necessity of change that must be brought about in the nature and disposition found there[43] and this dispositional change, man cannot bring about. Charnock found himself in good company as to the inability of man, and we find that he is pulling straight from the historical men of the Reformation as it concerns this doctrine. As noted by Peter Martyr Vermigli, the soul had "blinded itself but could not enlighten itself."[44] It is in this context that Charnock frames the definition of regeneration; he states:

> A supernatural renewing grace, must expel corrupt habits from the will, and reduce it to its true object. When faith is planted, it brings love to work by: when the soul is renewed, there is an harmony between God and the heart, between the mind and the word, between the will and the duty: when the appetite, and true taste of the soul, is restored in regeneration, then spring up strong desires to apply itself to every holy service.[45]

What is the foundational aspect of Charnock's concept of regeneration? It is to be found in the understanding of the enormity of God's grace, more specifically, God's renewing grace through the work of the Spirit, purchased by the blood of Christ. The concept of grace is pervasive in Charnock's doctrine of regeneration, and it has far-reaching implications throughout his system of thought. What is entailed in this "renewing

---

40. Van Asselt, *Reformed Thought of Freedom*, 121.

41. Van Asselt, *Reformed Thought of Freedom*, 121. "First, there is a reality in which there is only corruption... Secondly, there is a reality in which there is only holiness... Thirdly, there is a reality in which there is both corruption and holiness. In this reality man does the good and the bad. It is the state of regeneration (of man after conversion)."

42. Charnock, "God's Holiness," in *Works*, 2:235.

43. Charnock, *The Doctrine of Regeneration*, 6.

44. Vermigli, *Philosophical Works*, 4:316–17.

45. Charnock, *The Doctrine of Regeneration*, 46–47.

A SOUL FRAMED IN CHRIST

grace"? There is a great deal of weight, in Charnock's system of thought, to the concept (reality) of grace, and it is heavily integrated into his understanding of regeneration.

i. The Substantive Reality of Grace

We find the height of Charnock's definition of regeneration pressing the edges of reality and exposing the twofold situation: man's deplorable condition and the magnitude of God's grace. That is, regeneration "consists in a real change from nature to grace as well as by grace."[46] In case there is any question about this realness of this change, Charnock states emphatically that the "term of creation is real: the form introduced in the new creature, is as real as the form introduced by creation, into any being."[47] Why is this the case; rather, why must this be the case? For Charnock, the answer is simple: "Scripture terms manifest it so."[48]

It is the truth manifested in the Scriptures that provide a basis for expanding upon that fundamental reality contained in the work of regeneration. It is a new reality brought about in a new creation—a "divine nature, the image of God, a law put into the heart . . . It is a reality the soul partakes of; it gives a real denomination, a new man, a new heart, a new spirit, a new creature, something of a real existence; it is called a resurrection."[49]

Why does Charnock choose to cap this description with the emphatic: "It is called a resurrection"? What is the sum and substance of this resurrected creature, for Charnock? His selection of words, or word choice, is intentional and opting to employ, such words as "real," and "resurrection" is an effort to convey the reality of this redemptive work in Christ. So, "real," and "resurrection" are meant to further illustrate, not only the necessity of regeneration, the efficient of regeneration, and the instrument of regeneration, but also to draw man to the edges of his existence

---

46. Charnock, *The Doctrine of Regeneration*, 109.
47. Charnock, *The Doctrine of Regeneration*, 109.
48 Charnock, *The Doctrine of Regeneration*, 109.
49. Charnock, *The Doctrine of Regeneration*, 109. The necessity that Charnock speaks of the realness of this creation—it cannot be anything other than this "real existence." If it is other than this real existence, then the whole of his system would collapse or, perhaps, be nothing more than a fanciful construction of the mind that would produce nothing new in a life other than some meager explorations of man's deceptive imagination about what he cannot even correctly imagine himself capable of. It would be mere imagery without the substance—form without matter.

in either a state of depravity ("worse than nothing") or as a redeemed ("divine nature") child of God. Charnock goes to great lengths to establish the nature—the absolute magnificent redemptive work—of the triune God in bringing forth this new creature. For example, in the discourse, *The Chief Sinners Objects of the Choicest Mercy*, Charnock establishes the finer distinctions and draws parallels between God's creation *ex nihilo* and the creation of life out of death, in order to undergird the sum and substance of man's dark and confused soul. "His cresting power drew the world out of nothing," proclaims Charnock, "but his converting power frames the new creature out of something worse than nothing."[50]

This aspect of reality, especially that of a new creation, a resurrected creature, is significant because it axes the root of any contrived reality about who a man is in his depraved state. Charnock rightfully emphasizes the nature of this new creature being a "resurrection" or a resurrected creature. Most vividly, he depicts this new creature as being not merely a new creature, per se; rather, a new creature that has come forth from the Creator. Yet, this creation stands, if possible, apart and above all other creations that the Creator has brought forth. This new creation is depicted in the following words by Charnock:

> Grace, or a gracious man in respect of his grace, is called God's workmanship, Eph. 2:10, ποίημα, not ἔργον; work of his art as well as strength, and operation of his mind as well as his hand; his *poem*, not barely a work of omnipotency, but an intellectual spark. A new creature is a curious piece of divine art, fashioned by God's wisdom to set forth the praise of the framer, as a poem is, by a man's reason and fancy, to publish the wit and parts of the composer.[51]

Consider, for example, the foundational necessity of God's *creatio ex nihilio*, which is a doctrine that stands disputed throughout church history. Yet, if that doctrine is removed, the whole of Scripture to unravels—in essence doing what Adam and Eve sought to do in the Garden, supplant the seat of Christ. Such an act of creation is not something that goes unnoticed by Charnock; instead, he employs the magnificent aspect of *creatio ex nihilio* as the backdrop to illustrate the greater creative working power of God[52] in

---

50. Charnock, "The Chief Sinners Objects of the Choicest Mercy," in *Works*, 5:54.

51. Charnock, "The Chief Sinners Objects of the Choicest Mercy," in *Works*, 5:542.

52 This is an excellent depiction of God's creative work being foundational. However, for Charnock, the *creatio ex nihilio* was indeed the sovereign Creator calling things into existence, yet the more magnificent work of *creatio ex nihilio* was not in the Garden of

bringing forth a resurrected creature that was dead. "His creating power," says Charnock, "drew the world of out nothing." This "creating power" is a fundamental reality that impacts the relational reality between the Creator and the creature.[53] Yet, Charnock is only staging the greater reality of this glorious and gracious power of the Creator. Charnock continues, "His converting power frames the new creature out of something worse than nothing."[54] Making something out of "worse than nothing" is more significant than creation, as it brings light into the heart, and establishes it up despite all the opposition that the devil and a man's own corruption makes.[55] Why is it greater? It is greater because it is "a change of a nature hateful to God," Charnock asserts, "into a nature delightful to him, a corrupt creature into an holy one, a change of something worse than a bare creature into something like the great Creator and Redeemer."[56] The boundless power of God's redemptive grace, for Charnock, is the copiousness of a temporal and eternal exhibition, to the extent we can grasp, of the meritorious work of Christ to bring life from the deadness of unregenerate man.

So, for Charnock, any system that is to be built upon regeneration must do so with the fact that what unfolds in the soul of man is real! To emphasize the realness of this regenerational activity of grace, Charnock employs many descriptors to convey the realness. For example, it is real in its existence, repentance, punishment, enmity, and change. Also, the relationship is real, and there is real happiness, real intent, real feelings, real converts; the act of the mind is real. If this were not the situation, the implications would be the indubitable unraveling of the whole of what is contained in the reality of regeneration that was purchased by the blood of Christ. At the same time, if the foundation is anything less than real, it will not support the structure that is being erected on it. The notion of "realness" is Charnock's categorical approach to dealing with the content of conformity to the imitable perfections of God, more specifically, the supposition of continuity in that conformity.

Eden but in the desolate garden of the soul of man.

53. Elsewhere Charnock refers to this as the soul taking note of the workmanship of God (Eph 2:10). See Charnock, A Discourse upon the Wisdom of God, in *Works*, 3:59–60.

54 It appears that Charnock employs this phrase "worse than nothing" in several different areas, and each time it is in the context of all things fallen in comparison to a holy God. See Charnock, "A Discourse of the Efficient of Regeneration," in *Works*, 3:266.

55 Charnock, "The Chief Sinners Objects of the Choicest Mercy," in *Works*, 5:541.

56. Charnock, "A Discourse of the Nature of Regeneration," in *Works*, 3:153.

ii. The Substantial Being of Grace

If the conforming reality of this nature is grace, what does the being look like when it is exposed to this reality of grace? That is, what does Charnock perceive this reality to look like in a redeemed soul? There is the conforming aspect to the imitable perfections of God; however, what does the structure of the soul that contains this imitable perfection of God looks like? One might expect an in-depth metaphysical exploration of the concept of being, which would be a worthwhile exploration. However, that is not necessary for Charnock, because he managed to keep the entirety of that reality centralized in the reality of grace. So, if we were to ask Charnock what is the depth of the soul's metaphysical construct that has been regenerated and brought into this conformity of God, he would reply with a simple, yet absolutely fundamental defining aspect of that redeemed soul's reality. "Grace only," declares Charnock, "gives being to a Christian, and constitutes him so."[57]

To follow up on Charnock's simplified response to this metaphysical construct of the soul, one might ask: "What do you mean, "Grace only gives being to a Christian?" The response that would be offered up will only be the doubling down on the reality of grace, because for Charnock the fundamental defining aspect of a Christian is the grace of God—period. Furthermore, the realm of the soul is the place where the magnitude of God's grace and the reality of his grace define the existence, as well as the substantive reality, of the beauty that God impresses upon the soul in his redemptive work.

This substantive reality of grace in the soul is not a localized reality; instead, it is both comprehensive and permeates throughout the soul where the disposition as has been altered to function in its original design: redounding the glory of God. That is, this substantive reality of grace found in the beauty of a redeemed soul is indicative of the universality of grace, which is a constant in Charnock's thought. "All grace," Charnock declares, "is summed up in a conformity to God and Christ; for it is nothing but a restoration of the divine image, a reimplantation of that in the soul, which was defaced and lost by Adam . . . Every grace is a member and part of the divine image, and answers in some proportion to some imitable perfection of God."[58] Therefore, this life-shaping grace of God that brings conformity

---

57. Charnock, "The Necessity of Regeneration," in *Works*, 3:28.
58. Charnock, "A Discourse of the Knowledge of God," in *Works*, 4:34.

to the center of man's existence, as well as the totality of man's existence. This totality of life-shaping grace is manifold for Charnock, because it is identified, first, in the summation of the soul's conformity to Christ— "all grace is summed up in a conformity to God and Christ." Secondly, inherent within the summation of grace is the extent of that grace in the soul, which is the reality of grace contained in the soul's disposition. This life-shaping grace infiltrates the totality of the soul which once was defined by its depraved nature. "The proper seat of grace," says Charnock, "is the substance of the soul, and therefore it influences every faculty."[59] The influence of grace upon every human faculty is unavoidable in Charnock's mind, because it "is the form whence the perfection both of understanding and will do flow; it is not therefore placed in either of them, but in the essence of the soul . . . It is not one particular faculty that is perfected by grace, but the substance of the soul."[60] The summation of this conformity for Charnock is and must be rooted in grace, and this grace is the defining substance of the soul's disposition that reflects the glory of God; this reality is implicated throughout all faculties.

This multidimensional perspective (substantive and universal) on grace is a fundamental necessity, especially when one is attempting to convey or depict the glorious reality of this grace within the soul. This necessity, for Charnock, becomes evident as he demonstrates the internal framework of the reality of this being of grace. He approaches the soul with the understanding and conviction that the Creator, as a wise builder, "lays the foundation in sound habits, whereon to raise a superstructure of

---

59. Charnock, "A Discourse of the Nature of Regeneration," in *Works*, 3:96. Charnock references Suarez in this statement Suarez de Gratia, l. vi. c. 12; Num. 10:13–14.

60. Charnock, "A Discourse of the Nature of Regeneration," in *Works*, 3:96. Grace is a unified operation within the soul that infiltrates all the faculties, not just the understanding or the will. This very notion of grace selectively operating within one particular faculty is something that William Ames denounced. The thought that "true faith [is] partly in the understanding and partly in the will, is not quite correct," Ames points out, because true faith "is a single virtue and brings forth acts of one quality throughout, not partly of knowledge and partly of the affections, 1 Cor. 13." The unifying reality, for both the cognitive and volitional aspects of faith, is located in the "heart" for Ames. "The firm assent to the promises of the gospel," Ames notes, "is called both faith and trust, partly because, as general assent, it produces faith and partly because, as a special and firm assent, it flows from trust as it takes actual possession of grace already received. The firm assent leans on the trust of the heart as a middle or third term [argumentum], by the strength of which alone a conclusion about faith can be reached." See Ames, *The Marrow of Theology*, 83.

gracious actions."[61] On numerous occasions, Charnock will employ vivid imagery when attempting to come to grips with the reality of grace that is contained in the soul, and for him, it is best presented from an architectural perspective. For example, he talks about "Christ laying the foundation in grace, he will be in him rearing the superstructure to glory."[62] This "rearing the superstructure" is the work of the Holy Spirit that will "raise the superstructure upon that foundation Christ had already laid,"[63] and this work of the Spirit is necessary to the superstructure of saving faith.[64]

It is in this raising of the superstructure that Charnock directs the redeemed soul to the "most magnificent act of divine power that God ever put forth, viz., that in the resurrection of our Saviour, Eph. 1:19 . . . as great as all that power which is displayed in our redemption, from the first foundation to the last line in the superstructure."[65] The soundness and firmness of the foundation become readily apparent as Charnock works through the various facets of this superstructure that has been built within the redeemed soul. This is the reality of grace in the glorious work of the Trinity that defines the architectural structure of a soul. That is, the reality of this grace in the formative nature of being internally conformed to God's holiness—in the foundation of the soul, superstructure of the soul, and every line of the foundation and superstructure. It is an impossibility to erect a superstructure where there is no foundation to build that superstructure.

Grace is the life-shaping reality within the internal framework of a soul redeemed in Christ. However, is it possible that there is something more ultimate beneath this foundation of grace that brings the being of a Christian into existence and constitutes him so? There is, most definitely, another fundamental component of reality that defines the substance of this connectivity, as well as the nature of the conformity of the soul to the imitable perfections of God. For Charnock, the ultimacy of the preservation of this reality of grace in the superstructure within the soul is found in covenantal reality, more specifically, with "God in covenant." "He that hath laid the foundation," Charnock says, "can and will preserve the superstructure, not only because he formed it, but because he hath promised

---

61. Charnock, "A Discourse of the Efficient of Regeneration," in *Works*, 3:271.
62. Charnock, "A Discourse of God's Being the Author of Reconciliation," in *Works*, 3:468.
63. Charnock, "A Discourse of the Necessity of Christ's Exaltation," in *Works*, 5:79.
64 Charnock, "A Discourse of the Efficient of Regeneration," in *Works*, 3:229.
65. Charnock, "A Discourse Upon the Power of God," in *Works*, 2:159.

it."⁶⁶ This "because he hath promised" is a discerning characteristic of the superstructure that defines Charnock's theological framework. In addition, it exposes the foundation for his doctrine of regeneration. It is tethered to a scriptural principle of covenantal conformity, and this covenantal conformity is the ultimate substratum that allows the reality of grace to stand erected in a redeemed soul.

c. Covenantal Substratum of Conformity

Patrick Gillespie in his work *Ark of the Covenant Opened Or a Treatise upon the Covenant of Redemption,* sees the covenant of redemption as another demonstration that the notion of man's ability to rise above his own depravity is a fiction, with no grounding in reality. However, at the same time, it operated to make grace shine all the more in its efficacious work within the soul. "This covenant," Gillespie notes, "was necessary for cutting off all matter and occasion of self-glorification from man in his own redemption and salvation; for if the business of our Redemption and Salvation was transacted, concluded, done and ended betwixt Jehovah and Christ, without our knowledge or consent, before we had a Being; what have we to boast of?"⁶⁷ It is the ultimacy of the reality indicated in

---

66. Charnock, "A Discourse of the Church's Stability," in *Works,* 5:345.

67. Gillespie, *The Ark of the Covenant Opened Or the Secret of the Lord's Covenant Unsealed in a Treatise of the Covenant of Grace,* idem, *Ark of the Covenant Opened Or a Treatise upon the Covenant of Redemption,* 50. See also Trueman, *John Owen,* 72–73. During the period known as the High Orthodoxy, there is a particular doctrine that had taken center stage and had a profound impact on theology during this period of time. The doctrine that was being developed is known by different names, such as, the Latin term *"pactum salutis"* which is rendered in English as the "covenant of redemption" or "counsel of peace." Nonetheless, this was being developed because we see the adjustments made in *The Savoy Declaration* 1658 by a conference of English Congregationalist. More specifically, the language used in chapter 8.1 *Of Christ the Mediator,* "according to a covenant made between them both" and points out that the "first covenant made with man, was a covenant of works." This covenant would appear in some sense to be a rally point for many of the Puritans of that time, as well as, moving forward because the writing on this concept of the covenant of redemption was not scarce by any shape of the imagination. In his work, *A Heavenly Directory: Trinitarian Piety, Public Worship and a Reassessment of John Owen's Theology,* McGraw notes the following about the development of the covenant of redemption: "The general Reformed consensus that developed in the seventeenth century was that God the Father made an eternal covenant with his Son in order to redeem his elect. The Westminster Confession of Faith did not specify this eternal covenant explicitly." See Trueman, *John Owen Reformed Catholic, Renaissance Man,* 83. Truman further supports this point; in his work, *John Owen;* he indicates

this covenantal construct of our reality that Charnock identifies as the ultimate substratum of the new life in Christ.

It is with this in mind that we now turn to consider the covenant of redemption as it relates to the theological framework of Charnock. Specifically, how does the covenant of redemption functions as the ultimate substratum for Charnock's doctrine of regeneration?

The answer to the question mentioned above is both simple and complex. The simple response is that the same significance of this notion of covenant—expressed above—can be attributed to Charnock because the covenant of redemption functions as a substantial reality—a reality that shapes and defines Charnock's theology that is most noticeable in his *A Discourse on the Author of Reconciliation*. In this discourse, Charnock will demonstrate that the concept of "covenant" is just as important, if not more so, to a proper understanding of regeneration as any other aspect of our

---

that the concept of the covenant of redemption was present in Reformed theology even before the terminology was developed. John Calvin (1509–1564), *Institutes*, 3.21.5. Helm, in his article, *"Calvin and the Covenant: Unity and Continuity,"* 65–81. Helm has constructed evidence that demonstrates that there the fundamental characteristics of the covenant of redemption to be squarely rooted in the theological thought of John Calvin. See Clark, http://www.ligonier.org/learn/articles/history-covenant-theology/. Theodore Beza (1519–1605), Zacharias Ursinus (1534–1583), Caspar Olevianus, See Clark, *Caspar Olevian and the Substance of the Covenant, The Double Benefit of Christ*, 178. Rollock (1555–1559), *Selected Works of Robert Rollock*, 1:31–61. William Ames (1576–1633); see Van Vliet, *Studies in Christian History and Thought, The Rise of Reformed System, The Intellectual Heritage of William Ames*, 31. Dickson (1583–1662), *The Sum of Saving Knowledge: Or, A Brief Sum of Christian Doctrine*. Preston (1587–1628), *The New Covenant or The Saints Portion*, 374–75. Rutherford (1600–1661), *Covenant of Life Opened: Or, A Treatise of the Covenant of Grace*, 330–31. Coceius, *The Doctrine of the Covenant and Testament of God*, vol. 3, *Classic Reformed Theology*. Gillespie (1617–1675), *Ark of the Covenant Opened Or a Treatise upon the Covenant of Redemption*. Jacombs (1623–1687), *Morning Exercise Methodized*, 218–19. Francis Turretin offers a Scriptural basis for the covenant between the Father and the Son. See Turretin, *Institutes of Elenctic Theology*, 3:175–78. Owen (1625–1699), *Hebrews*, vol. 3. Bagshawe (1628–1702), *Essays on Union to Christ*, 262. Charnock (1628–1680), *The Works of Stephen Charnock*, vol. 4. Flavel (1639–1691), "Opens the Covenant of Redemption betwixt the Father and the Redeemer," in *Works*, 1:52. Witsius (1636–1708), *The Economy of the Covenants between God and Man*, 1:177–91. Willard (1640–1707), *A Compleat Body of Divinity in Two Hundred and Fifty Expository Lectures on the Assembly's Shorter Catechism*, 275–313. Traill (1642–1716), *The Works of Robert Traill*, "Vindication of the Protestant Doctrine Concerning Justification, and of its Preachers and professors, from the Unjust Charge of Antinomianism," 1:280–321. Vanderkemp (1664–1718), *The Christian Entirely the Property of Christ, in Life and Death: Exhibited in Fifty-Three Sermons on the Heidelberg Catechism*, 1:129, 261, 391. See Edwards (1703–1758), *Observations Concerning the Scripture Trinity of the Trinity and Covenant of Redemption*.

theological construct, at least this is the case for Charnock. What is more interesting is the place that we find the highest concentration of the word "covenant"—volume 3, pertaining to the doctrine of regeneration. For example, the word "regeneration" is used some 389 times in volume 3 of his discourses on regeneration, and the word "covenant" is used 369 times in the same volume. This serves to illustrate the significance, to some extent, of the two concepts that must be necessarily integrated into Charnock's understanding of the structure of the doctrine of regeneration.

Charnock devotes a good portion of his sermon on *God the Author of Reconciliation*, an exposition of 2 Cor 5:18–19 which reads, "And all things *are* of God, who hath reconciled us to himself by Jesus Christ, and hath given to us the ministry of reconciliation; to wit, that God was in Christ, reconciling the world unto himself, not imputing their trespasses unto them; and hath committed unto us the word of reconciliation."[68] This passage is employed to ground the reality of regeneration within the eternal realm of the covenant of redemption. It is within this grounding of regeneration that Charnock draws out the vital elements within the context of reconciliation: first, the notion of reconciliation which he identifies as foundational to regeneration; second, the notion that the covenant of redemption is tethered to Charnock's understanding of proper knowledge—eternal life.

As to regeneration, in the opening of this particular sermon Charnock identifies the covenantal nature of reconciliation in the redemptive work of Christ. This reconciliation is what Charnock sums up as a "copy of God's heart from eternity," which speaks to the vastness of God's redemption that is identified in the covenant of redemption. "The Father enters into terms of agreement with the Son," says Charnock, "about the work and methods of redemption, which is expressed by divines by the term covenant."[69]

This regenerational foundation that Charnock tethers to reconciliation is identified as such because the fruits of this reconciliation are manifested in the Spirit's mission. "The great end why the Spirit was sent," says Charnock, "was to manifest this acceptance; to evidence to the world that Christ was no impostor, because he was gone to the Father, John 16:7–10,

---

68. Second Cor 5:18–19 electronic ed. of the 1769 edition of the 1611 Authorized Version.

69. Charnock, "A Discourse of God's Being the Author of Reconciliation," in *Works*, 3:371.

and had a welcome in heaven."⁷⁰ Furthermore, as a result of the covenantal nature of the "work and methods of redemption," Charnock notes:

> There was no error or mistake in any part of the management of this work on Christ's part; for the Spirit is not sent to rectify anything, but to raise the superstructure upon that foundation Christ had already laid. He was to declare only what he heard, John 16:13, 14; to act the part of a minister to Christ, as Christ had acted the part of a minister to his Father; to glorify Christ, to manifest the fulness of his merit, and the benefits of his purchase; for he was to receive of Christ, *i.e.* the things of Christ, his truth and his grace, and manifest it to their souls, and imprint upon them the comfort of both.⁷¹

That raising of the superstructure is not only grounded in the covenantal reality of the redemptive work of Christ, but it is also the result of that redemptive work. This superstructure is Charnock's way of speaking to the internal framing within the soul which is the deconstruction of the old man and the construction of the new. He states: "It bears proportion to corruption. As sin expelled the whole frame of original righteousness, so regenerating grace expels the whole frame of original corruption."⁷² This "frame of original righteousness" is indicative of the necessity of righteousness before and after the fall, "continually necessary from the first moment of the fall,"⁷³ says Charnock. Hence, it is clearly stated that this passage of scripture (2 Cor 5:18–19) represents the "doctrine of redemption under the term of reconciliation" and this reconciliation by Christ, Charnock declares is "the foundation of the regeneration of nature; ver. 17, 18, 'All things are become new, and all things are of God who hath reconciled us to himself by Jesus Christ.'"⁷⁴ Yet, behind all of this stands that agreement between the Father and the Son in eternity, and it is there that the regenerate are identified prior to them becoming regenerate. "All the seed of Christ," says Charnock, "are in the covenant of redemption before they are regenerate, but not actually in the covenant of grace, and

---

70. Charnock, "A Discourse of God's Being the Author of Reconciliation," in *Works*, 3:427.

71. Charnock, "A Discourse of God's Being the Author of Reconciliation," in *Works*, 3:428.

72. Charnock, "A Discourse of the Nature of Regeneration," in *Works*, 3:96.

73. Charnock, "The Necessity of Regeneration," in *Works*, 3:19–20.

74. Charnock, "A Discourse of God's Being the Author of Reconciliation," in *Works*, 3:340.

under the influence of the special benefits of it, till they are regenerate; as all mankind were in the loins of Adam, but not guilty of his pollution till their natural generation."[75] The reality contained in the soul's renewal to the image of God through the redemptive work of Christ is an interlaced reality that is associated with both covenants—covenant of redemption and covenant of grace—which Charnock identifies in two different aspects of the salvific reality which speaks to the covenants. For example, Charnock further explains that the "salvation of the seed . . . is promised to the believer upon his faith; it is promised to Christ in behalf of the seed upon his suffering." Therefore, Charnock concludes that "the covenant of redemption is the foundation of the covenant of grace."[76]

Indeed, the tethering point of these covenants is squarely placed upon the sum and substance of Christ suffering, as well as the fact that "in the covenant of grace, Christ, or God in Christ, is the object of faith."[77] If this were not the case, in Charnock's mind, the covenants would be disjointed. However, Charnock reasons that Christ could not be the object of faith, "had not such an agreement between the Father and the Son preceded" in the covenant of redemption.[78] Not only is the "object of faith" defined in the covenant of redemption, but the "everlastingness of the covenant of grace depends upon the perpetuity of the covenant of redemption."[79] Furthermore, Charnock emphasizes that the validity of all that is associated with Christ's suffering, which finds its validity in the covenant of redemption. "All the promises," says Charnock, "as established by his death are yea and amen in him: they receive their validity from his death, and his death receives its validity from the covenant of redemption."[80] Not only the validation of his death but it is also the grounding factor of faith and hope which are tethered to the covenant of redemption, because the "hope believers have of eternal

---

75. Charnock, "A Discourse of God's Being the Author of Reconciliation," in *Works*, 3:376.

76. Charnock, "A Discourse of God's Being the Author of Reconciliation," in *Works*, 3:376.

77. Charnock, "A Discourse of God's Being the Author of Reconciliation," in *Works*, 3:376.

78. Charnock, "A Discourse of God's Being the Author of Reconciliation," in *Works*, 3:376.

79. Charnock, "A Discourse of God's Being the Author of Reconciliation," in *Works*, 3:376.

80. Charnock, "A Discourse of God's Being the Author of Reconciliation," in *Works*, 3:376.

life springs up originally from that promise made by the Father to the Son before the foundation of the world; for the promises of the covenant of grace were included in this covenant of redemption."[81]

Charnock depicts the connectivity of the covenant of redemption and the redemptive work of Christ in the following summative statement that speaks to the reality of this covenant connectivity and the manifestation of that connectivity in the new creature. Consider the following succinct statement of this cohesive covenantal reality which transition from the nature of the covenant of redemption to the covenant of grace. "He suffered himself to be pierced to death," Charnock notes, "that sin, the enemy of God's purity, might be destroyed."[82] And in this destroying of God's enemy, "the honour of the law, the image of God's holiness, might be repaired and fulfilled in the fallen creature."[83] That is, Christ in his suffering "restored the credit of divine holiness in the world, in manifesting by his death God an irreconcilable enemy to all sin, in abolishing the empire of sin, so hateful to God."[84] And that Christ, in his suffering, would restore "the rectitude of nature, and new framing the image of God in his chosen ones."[85]

However, this is not the only place that the covenant of redemption plays a vital role in the reality of regeneration. For example, Charnock in *The Knowledge of God* will continually tether a proper knowledge (eternal life) to this covenant as he establishes it in his *Discourse of the Knowledge of God*.[86] In this section, we see the connective lines of thought, for

---

81. Charnock, "A Discourse of God's Being the Author of Reconciliation," in *Works*, 3:376–77.

82. Charnock, "A Discourse upon the Holiness of God," in *Works*, 2:213.

83. Charnock, "A Discourse upon the Holiness of God," in *Works*, 2:213.

84. Charnock, "A Discourse upon the Holiness of God," in *Works*, 2:213.

85. Charnock, "A Discourse upon the Holiness of God," in *Works*, 2:213.

86. It is important to note that Charnock is not equating knowledge to eternal life, at least, not directly. However, this is where Charnock is dialing in the intrinsic relationship between knowledge of God and the conformity of that knowledge in the heart of man. Charnock does see this knowledge as a causation of eternal life. That is, "it is the effect for the cause;" says Charnock, "the knowledge of God is not formally eternal life, but the cause of it, and the antecedent means to it." He further clarifies this antecedent nature of the knowledge of God and notes that it "is not eternal life in the formality and nature of it, but in the infallibility of causation." His rationale for this position follows: "because if men had the true knowledge of Christ impressed upon them," Charnock reasons, "it could not be but they must believe in him, and consequently have both a right to eternal life and the fortaste of it." This is, for Charnock, a further delineation between knowledge of God and the saving knowledge of God and the latter is sure to be accompanied with "ardent love to him" and "cordial trust in him." Therefore, the saving causation of God's

Charnock, in his *Discourse on the Author of Reconciliation*. The latter being inundated with covenantal language and the heaviest concentration of the actual phrase "covenant of redemption." Although Charnock does not use the "covenant of redemption" phrase in the former discourse, nonetheless, he makes clear the necessity of this covenant and the reality of eternal life which is found in the knowledge of God and Christ. For Charnock, the glorious reality which is found in a soul that has been brought to life from death is connected to the covenant relation between the Father and the Son before time began. "He is therefore," asserts Charnock, "said to know his sheep, John 10.14 (every one in particular, as he knows the stars by name); otherwise the foundation of the Lord, this covenant of redemption, which is the foundation of all his proceedings, could not stand sure."[87] If this covenantal foundation were to unravel, the whole construct of our eternal life would be subjected to this fraying nature of reality. The reason for this fraying of reality is because, according to Charnock, the truth of life, the knowledge of eternal life, is wrapped up in the covenant between God and Christ—so much so that truth itself would cease to exist if God were to fail to perform the promises given to Christ in the covenant of redemption. "The ground," asserts Charnock, "where of is particularly the veracity and faithfulness of God in his promises, and the truth of God in his primes to man is founded upon the truth of God in performing his covenant with Christ."[88]

Charnock tethers the knowledge of God that results in eternal life within the reality of the covenant of redemption. In his *Discourse on The Knowledge of God*, he states that "the knowledge of the Son is made a cause of eternal life, as well as the knowledge of the Father."[89] Charnock continues this line of thinking and notes "that the true God may refer to the veracity of God the Father in his covenant with Christ, and his promises to us,"[90]

---

knowledge is when the knowledge of God "descends from the head to the heart, which is light in the mind and heart in the affections; such a knowledge of God as includes faith in him." See Charnock, "A Discourse of the Knowledge of God," in *Works*, 4:10.

87. Charnock, "A Discourse of God's Being the Author of Reconciliation," in *Works*, 3:385.

88. Charnock, "The Knowledge of God," in *Works*, 4:13. We hear echoes of William Perkins in Charnock's covenantal reality.

89. Charnock, "The Knowledge of God," in *Works*, 4:13.

90. Charnock, "The Knowledge of God," in *Works*, 4:13. This veracity of God is a fundamental necessity for the covenant to be a covenant, as well as for faith to have a proper object. As Charnock points out, it is not one particular attribute of God that

which he points out the Syriac translation: "To know thee to be the only God of truth."[91] So, for Charnock, this directly grounds this knowing, the fiducial aspect of knowledge. This "knowledge [is] accompanied with faith and trust in God, the ground whereof is particularly the veracity and faithfulness of God in his promise; and the truth of God in his promise to

---

functions as the first object of faith; rather, the grounding factor or object of faith is directly tethered to the veracity of God. "Particularly," says Charnock, "the veracity of God is the first object or ground of faith. He is not the first object of faith in any attribute, but his veracity. As God creates the world as powerful, and punisheth the wicked as he is just, and pardons sin as he is merciful, and provides for all as he is good, so he is believed on as true in the first motion of the soul to him." Hence, the grounding of eternal life covenantally, that is, according to Charnock, the "first act of faith considers God as true in his promise, and powerful to accomplish it: 'This is life eternal, to know thee, the only true God, and Jesus Christ whom thou hast sent,' John 17:3. Ἀληθινός, signifies *verax*, as well as *verus*; not only true in thy nature, but true in thy word; ' the only true God' in Jesus Christ, in whom there was the performance of the first and greatest promise made in paradise; by the same figure spoken of before, ἕν διὰ δυοῖν." See Charnock, "A Discourse of the Object of Faith," 5:152. Similarly, "The veracity and faithfulness of a God in Christ, pawned in the promise," Ebenezer Erskine points out, "is another ground upon which faith builds . . . that our faith cannot subsist without faithfulness in God." See Erskine, *The Whole Works of the Late Rev. Ebenezer Erskine*, 1:241. John Owen connects God's authority with his veracity in revealing the object of our faith. "The *authority* and *veracity* of God revealing the material object of our faith, or what it is our duty to believe," Owen says, "are the formal object and reason of our faith, from whence it ariseth and whereinto it is ultimately resolved—that is, the only reason why we do believe that Jesus Christ is the Son of God, that God is one single essence subsisting in three persons, is because that God who is truth, the "God of truth," Deut 32:4, who 'cannot lie,' Tit 1:2, and whose 'word is truth,' John 17:17, and the Spirit which gave it out is 'truth,' 1 John 5:6, hath revealed these things to be so. And our believing these things on that ground renders our faith *divine and supernatural*; supposing also a respect unto the subjective efficiency of the Holy Ghost inspiring it into our minds, whereof afterwards: or, to speak distinctly, our faith is *supernatural*, with respect unto the production of it in our minds by the Holy Ghost; and *infallible*, with respect unto the formal reason of it, which is divine revelation; and is *divine*, in opposition unto what is merely human, on both accounts." See Owen, "The Reason of Faith," in *Works*, 4:18. Thomas Manton divides and defines this "authority and veracity of God." According to Manton, first, it is the authority of God by which "God commandeth men to repent; charge the heart in the name of God, as it will answer to him another day." Secondly, it is the veracity of God that constitutes these things true. See Manton, *The Complete Works of Thomas Manton*, 17:370. For Ezekiel Hopkins, the very notion of the authority and veracity of God speaks to what he identifies as a "dogmatical faith." "I call that," says Hopkins, "which hath for its object the whole revealed truth of God: and it is nothing but a firm, undoubting assent to the verity and certainty of whatever is contained in the Holy Scriptures; upon no other account and reason, than merely the authority and veracity of God, who is the author of it. See Hopkins and Pratt, *The Works of the Right Reverend Father in God, Ezekiel Hopkins*, 3:465–66.

91. Charnock, "The Knowledge of God," in *Works*, 4:13.

man is founded upon the truth of God in performing his covenant with Christ."[92] Charnock directly ties this together in this discourse and furthers the thought in his *Discourse on the Author of Reconciliation*, where the notion of covenant shows up in a significant manner, so much so that if you were to remove the word "covenant" from that particular discourse, it would probably be incoherent. The framework in its entirety is built upon the concept of covenant and the covenant of redemption.[93]

92. Charnock, "The Knowledge of God," in *Works*, 4:13. Charnock uses this phrase "veracity and faithfulness" only twice. Once in the discourse mentioned above, where it is a fundamental aspect of the covenantal reality of redemption and eternal life. The second use of the phrase, "veracity and faithfulness," is used in *The Necessity of Regeneration*, where Charnock, once again, ties the covenantal reality to God's "veracity and faithfulness," more specifically, the righteousness whereby God is granting his children the crown of glory. "But it is the veracity and faithfulness of God which is meant by righteousness there, and otherwhere in Scripture. It is a justice due to the promise, not to the nature of the grace, and due to the covenant made with Christ, which was, that he should have a seed to serve him; upon which compact our Saviour so peremptorily demands his people's being with him in glory: John 17:24, 'Father, I will that they also whom thou hast given me be with me where I am.' As much as to say, Father, I will not remit a tittle of that article, which is part of the covenant between thee and me; I will have that performed to the full."

93. The number of direct references to the word "covenant" is astounding, and it is used 257 times throughout. In addition to the word "covenant," Charnock uses "covenant of redemption" 29 times in this same discourse. The notion of the "covenant of redemption" is expressed by different words: "agreement with" is used roughly 12 times in this discourse; the word "compact" is used some 12 times in this same discourse, and the phrase "Father covenants with Christ" is used once. The Latin use of *pactum salutis* for the "covenant of redemption" is not found in Charnock's works. Similar phrases or terms are used throughout by Charnock that would express the same thing as "covenant of redemption." For example, Charnock also uses an "agreement between" approximately 33 times and does use "Father covenants with Christ," and "compact." Charnock's use of the covenant reality has garnered some criticism suggesting the covenant of redemption is a potential gateway to an unscriptural territory. The "elaboration of the theology of the covenants by Charnock," says Tudur Jones, "exemplifies the tendency to move beyond the testimony of Scripture into the realm of scholasticism." See Jones, "Union with Christ: The Existential Nerve of Puritan Piety," 186–208. Jones is not alone in sounding the alarm of the "potential" dangers of the concept of the covenant of redemption. For example, Karl Barth suggests that the notion is an absurdity when he poses the following question: "Can we really think of the first and second persons of the triune Godhead as two divine subjects and therefore as two legal subjects who can have dealings and enter into obligations one with another?" See Barth, *Church Dogmatics: The Doctrine of God*, 4:65. O. Palmer Robertson claims that there is no historical basis for this concept and that there was "no specific development in the classic creeds of the Reformers of the sixteenth and seventeenth centuries." See his: *The Christ of the Covenants*, 54. Robert Letham expresses his concern in more harsh terms, "The doctrine of the Trinity should

V

The Epistemological Strands of Conformity

As we have seen in the previous section, for Charnock, there is this reticulating aspect to the reality of the soul, that is, there is a comprehensive network that lays as the backdrop for the soul, whether it is depraved or redeemed. For example, man was created in the image of God; by default, this placed man in a Creator-creature relationship, and man was so designed to redound the imitable perfections of God. Inherent within this relationship of conformity of the soul to these imitable perfections, there is seated the notion of capacity. It would seem rather odd for God to have created man with the command to glorify him and be conformable to the imitable perfections of God, yet not have the capacity to do so.[1] This reality of conformity, therefore, brings us to consider Charnock's capacious epistemological nature of the soul.[2]

---

have provided a barrier against the idea of the covenant of Redemption . . . to describe the relations of the three persons in the Trinity as a covenant, or to affirm that there was a need for them to enter into covenantal—even contractual—arrangements is to open the door to heresy." See his: *The Westminster Assembly: Readings Its Theology in Historical Context*, 236, and especially pages 194–95. T. F. Torrance expresses a similar concern as Jones and identifies the concept of the covenant of redemption in the Puritan theology as being abstract; see his *The School of Faith: the Catechisms of the Reformed Church*, lxxix.

1. Although it goes without saying, we are not speaking in terms of an ability of man to do something on his own and this should be readily apparent by this point of the paper, especially considering the principle of contrariety that is found in Charnock's theological system of thought.

2. Charnock, "A Discourse upon God's Being a Spirit," in *Works*, 1:165, 273. Throughout Puritan writings, numerous descriptive phrases attempt to capture this

Charnock spends a good deal of time on developing what I will refer to as epistemological strands.[3] For example, Charnock divides knowledge into four strands: speculative, practical, experimental, and knowledge of interest, and proceeds to show the nature of these different types of knowledge and how they are intertwined.[4] There is a tight correlation between Charnock's knowledge of God and the transition from the corrupt nature of man to man in nature (state) of grace (regeneration) and he will on different occasions speak of this in terms of capacity.

Implicit with this notion of conformity is the realization of a new capacity that accompanies this conformity to God's imitable perfections; that is, the deformity of man has been removed. Charnock draws out the parallel of this unique relationship between conformity and capacity: "Is it not our highest excellency to be conformed to God in holiness, in as full a measure as our finite natures are capable,"[5] asks Charnock? What does

---

capacious reality of the soul. However, it seems that Flavel is more expressive of the soul's capacity and carries the most imagery as found in his sermon on Mathew 16:26. "No other soul," says Flavel, "besides man's is marriageable to Christ, or capable of espousals to the King of glory: they were not designed, and therefore not endued with a capacity for such an honour as this: but such a capacity hath every soul." See Flavel, "A Treatise on the Soul of Man," in *Works*, 3:158. Richard Baxter identifies this capacity with the soul's nobility. "How noble a nature is that which is capable of knowing not only all things in the world, (in its measure), but God himself, and the things of the world that is to come; and capable of loving and enjoying God, and of seeking and serving him in order to that enjoyment!" See Baxter, *The Practical Works of the Rev. Richard Baxter*, 18:14–15. John Howe sees a comprehensive reality contained in this capacity of the soul. Howe states that the "great Creator and Author of all things should frame a creature of so vast comprehension as the spirit of man, put into it a capacity of knowing and conversing with himself, give it some prospect of his own glory and blessedness." See Howe, *The Works of the Reverend John Howe*, 2:10.

3. I refer to these four kinds of knowledge as "epistemological strands" because Charnock treats them as such. That is, he will identify the "speculative" epistemological strand as one that can exist by itself; however, this same strand is necessitated for the others to be what they are.

4. Siekawitch, *Balancing Head and Heart*.

5. Charnock, "A Discourse of the Sinfulness and Cure of Thought," in *Works*, 5:303. This notion of capacity, an intrinsic element of conformity, in the context of conformity, gives us insight into what Charnock perceives to be the range of this reality, especially in this temporal realm and that which is contained in the eternal realm of glory. Nonetheless, not just that there is a capacity to be conformed to God's holiness, but to do so in a full measure of that capacity. This does reveal the inner heart of this Puritan and allows us to understand what he was attempting to do in his various discourses. That is, explore what the content of this "full measure" should look like in this finite nature. The extension of this capacity or ability has the restrictions removed by the reality of grace, to the

it mean for something too have the capacity for something? Is capacity to be understood as a limitation, or should it be taken to speak to the height of an ability to do something?[6] For Charnock, it would seem that capacity is to be considered in light of the height of ability, which is intimated in the fullest measure of our capacity in our finite nature. Does this not speak to the grace that removes the limiting nature contained within capacity (of deformity), in order that we might speak to the heightened ability when grace is the foundation, structure, as well as the superstructure of the soul? So, there is intrinsically within the notion of capacity both a limiting and delimiting component. For example, in man's deformity there is a capacity to do that which is not in accord with God creating man in his image, as well as an incapacity to do that which it was created to do—glorify the Creator. In the same manner, when the soul has been redeemed in Christ, there is a capacity associated with man's conformity, which is the ability to redound the glory of God.

John Flavel in his *A Treatise of the Soul of Man* has much to say about the capacious nature of the soul that God has created in his image, more specifically, the capacious epistemological nature of this soul. "Let the ignorant consider," says Flavel,

> God hath created their souls with a capacity of knowing him and enjoying him as well as others that are famed in the world for knowledge and wisdom. *There is a spirit in man, and the inspiration of the Almighty giveth them understanding.* The faculty is in man, but the wisdom and knowledge that enlightens is from God; as the dial shews the hour of the day when the sun-beams fall upon it.[7]

---

extent possible, which comes in and reframes the internal stature of the soul.

6. The capacity of something can be viewed as a limiting facet of its nature; however, it can also speak to the design by which it is meant to function. Either way, there are defining aspects of this capacity, which Charnock has been establishing throughout his discourses. This nature suggests that there are degrees of capacity, and these degrees are defined, based off what something finds itself conforming or deforming to. Secondly, within that realm of conformity, there is another degree of capacity that will define the nature of that thing. In his case, as we have been considering man, it would mean that in man's deformed position he is not capable—no spiritual capacity. He cannot change his state of depravity; he cannot redeem himself; he cannot come to a saving knowledge of God. However, on the other hand, the capacious nature of the soul is redefined when it is redeemed and has been brought into conformity with the holiness of God.

7. Flavel, *The Whole Works of the Reverend John Flavel*, 3:188. Flavel is one of those Puritans who is fascinated with the soul and its capacity.

A SOUL FRAMED IN CHRIST

Charnock acknowledges what Flavel has identified in the fact that "God hath created their souls with a capacity of knowing him" to be a relational aspect of epistemology—conformity and capacity—that functions as a structure which manifests the dynamic nature of that relationship between God as the Creator or God as the Redeemer. It is the knowledge of the Redeemer, a saving knowledge, that Charnock sets out to distinguish while at the same time establishing the fullness of that redeeming knowledge in what he calls the "properties of this knowledge."[8] For Charnock, these properties of knowledge, for Charnock, are indicative of the conformity to or deformity from those imitable perfections of God.

So, what is meant by the capacious epistemological nature of the soul? It is for Charnock a means of expressing the relational reality between conformity and the correlative capacity inherent within that conformity. For example, the "knowledge of God and Christ which is saving," contends Charnock, "differs not from other knowledge in regard of the object, but the manner of knowing and the effects of knowledge."[9] This distinguishing aspect of knowledge suggests that one "knows by a natural understanding, and knows God in the Scripture as he would know a thing

---

8. Charnock, "A Discourse of the Knowledge of God," in *Works*, 4:15. Thomas Brooks in his, "A Serious Discourse, Touching a Well-Grounded Assurance," lists 8 properties which accompanies saving knowledge: 1. working knowledge, an operative knowledge, 2. transforming knowledge, metamorphosing knowledge, 3. experimental knowledge, 4. heart-affecting knowledge, 5. world-crucifying, and a world-contemning knowledge, 6. soul-abasing, soul-humbling knowledge, 7. appropriating knowledge, 8. accompanied and attended: holy endeavors, and with heavenly desires, thirstings, and pantings after further knowledge of God, holy endeavors to edify others, holy zeal, and faith and confidence. See Brooks, "A Serious Discourse, Touching a Well-Grounded Assurance," in *Works*, 2:433–45.

9. Charnock, "A Discourse of the Knowledge of God," in *Works*, 4:41. I think this is where we see the Cambridge Platonist coming out in Charnock, especially in dealing with the relation between the subject and the object. Consider the similarity in the between Charnock and the words of Plato. See *Plato's Epistles*, 240–41. Although, it could suggest that Charnock is more of a hybrid of a Cambridge Platonist and a Calvinist Thomistic. Perhaps, along the lines of Augustine who noted that "the truest philosophy, in my opinion—has been crystallized through multifarious disputes throughout many centuries, because the times did not lack men of the utmost discernment and industry who, in their disputations, continued to teach that Aristotle and Plato blend and chord in such a manner that to the inattentive and unskilled they seem to be out of harmony." See Augustine, *The Happy Life and Answer to Skeptics and Divine Providence and the Problem of Evil and Soliloquies*, vol. 5. The Fathers of the Church, 219. See Cicero, *Academ.* 1.4.17 ff.; 2.5.15. See also, Tkacz, Aristotle, Augustine's Knowledge of, in *Augustine through the Ages: An Encyclopedia*, 58.

written in any other book"; however, "the other knowledge," according to Charnock, "is by an understanding opened to take in more fully what is presented."[10] This is the very nature of spiritual knowledge of God, which by design will "put an edge upon the appetite, and open the understanding wider, that it may be fill with more." [11]

Charnock's way of connecting the reality of conformity of the soul with the capacious epistemological nature is related to the fact that the "understanding [is] opened to take in more fully what is presented."[12] That is, knowledge is transforming, "which doth necessarily include a conformity to the object"[13] and in conforming to the object, there is a desire for more capacity to understand that conformity[14] which is related to the enlightenment of the capacious epistemological nature of the soul. Charnock states:

> When Christ is made known in them the hope of glory, as well as to them; when the knowledge of God in his grace, and the history of Christ in his nature, offices, and passion, is turned into an image and stamp, working the heart into its own form . . . In the saving knowledge, the notions of God in his gospel discovery, and of Christ in his mediation, are manifest in the heart, insinuating

---

10. Charnock, "A Discourse of the Knowledge of God," in *Works*, 4:41. Charnock employs a similar relation between conformity and the notion of capacity in *A Discourse upon the Holiness of God*. For example, there is a correlative aspect of conformity to the holiness of God and our capacity to partake in that holiness. "What life is to the body," Charnock says, "that is righteousness to the Spirit; and the greater measure of holiness it hath, the more of life it hath." Why is this the case? It is because, "in a greater nearness, and partakes more fully of the fountain of life." As a result, we are fitted for communion with God, since it is our beauty and our life, without it, what communion can an excellent God have with deformed creatures, a living God with dead creatures?" See Charnock, "A Discourse upon the Holiness of God," in *Works*, 2:270.

11. Charnock, "A Discourse of the Knowledge of God," in *Works*, 4:60. Charnock points out a little further down in the same section that this opening of the understanding is consistent with the spirit of knowledge that "the apostle prays for further perfection in the knowledge of Christ, and a fuller opening the eyes of their understandings to get into his secret things, and behold more of his glory. It is as natural for a saving knowledge to press to further attainments, as it is for a counterfeit knowledge to flag in its pursuit."

12. Charnock, "A Discourse of the Knowledge of God," in *Works*, 4:41.

13. Charnock, "A Discourse of the Knowledge of God," in *Works*, 4:42.

14. Charnock, "A Discourse in Self-Examination," in *Works*, 4:492. We see this opening of understanding in David in Ps 139:21–23 where he ransacks his heart and "begs of God to open his heart more fully to his knowledge, and bless him with a perfect discovery."

themselves secretly into the inward parts of the soul, and moulding the heart into the form of the evangelical doctrine.[15]

So it is, this evangelical reality that changes the whole frame of man, and this change is radical. For example, "this knowledge is enlightening, it is the image of God in the mind; when it is enlivening it is the image of God in the heart; a picture of God and Christ, drawn in the understanding, which enamors the will, and assimilates the whole soul to God. The gospel is this glass, which doth not only represent the object, but alters the complexion of the soul."[16] The altering glass of the gospel is a necessity because if Christ is formed in the head, then the notions of the mind must change and all of this "is in order to a Christ formed in the heart." [17] Therefore, the work of Christ in conforming the soul not only puts in man the capacity for grace but also the capacity for the saving knowledge of God,[18] and this saving knowledge, according to Charnock, "is a knowledge of a reality in God and Christ."[19] It is fitting that Charnock would use such language of capacity, because his notion of capacity is congruous with his notion of conformity, especially as it pertains to the knowledge of God.

a. Capacitating Nature of Conformity

The aforementioned raises a couple of questions: Is there an implicit relation between our epistemological capacity and the principle of conformity, especially the conformity of the image of God's holiness? If so, how does Charnock perceive this relation between epistemological capacity and the principle of conformity? Is it implicit within the principle of conformity? It is so by the very design of the soul in that God has created man in his image. In response to the question: "How did God create man?" Charnock's perspective is in agreement with the answer provided by the *Shorter Catechism*: "God created man male and female, after his own image, in knowledge, righteousness, and holiness, with dominion over the creatures."[20] So, in the

---

15. Charnock, "A Discourse of the Knowledge of God," in *Works*, 4:42.
16. Charnock, "A Discourse of the Knowledge of God," in *Works*, 4:43.
17. Charnock, "A Discourse of the Knowledge of God," in *Works*, 4:43.
18. Charnock, "A Discourse of the Knowledge of God," in *Works*, 4:30.
19. Charnock, "A Discourse of the Knowledge of God," in *Works*, 4:45.
20. Westminster Assembly, *The Westminster Confession of Faith*, 389. The scriptural support listed: Gen 1:26–28. And God said, Let us make man in our image, after our likeness: and let them have dominion over the fish of the sea, and over the fowl of the air,

work of regeneration there is the operation of spiritual conformity to the image of God, inherently built within this operation, if you will, which is the capacitating aspect of conformity—the knowledge of God.

What part does this relation of capacity and conformity play in Charnock's theory of knowledge? This relation functions as a connective aspect of man's reality about the principle of conformity, more specifically, the capacitating nature of that conformity to the imitable perfections of God that are identified in the epistemological construct of a new creature in Christ where "He shines in the capacity of our souls."[21] The intrinsic facet of this capacitating nature contained within that conformity to God is the very definable aspect of man's existence. More specifically, his epistemological environment, as it pertains to the image of God, and this epistemological environment, for Charnock, are intractably intertwined. That is, as "error in knowledge was the first deformity of man, and the cause of all the rest," says Charnock, "so the first line of conformity that the Spirit draws upon the soul, whence, as from the first matter, all those beautiful graces that appear in every region of the soul are formed."[22]

It would be a foreign concept in Charnock's mind to have such newness of life, conformity to the imitable perfections of Christ, and have a lack of thirst for knowledge of God.[23] The very reality of conformity brings with it a foreign capacity, an incapacity, in the depraved nature, so as a result "that soul," posits Charnock, "that is truly God-like aspires to as high a knowledge of him as the creature is capable of."[24] Here again, we find Charnock exploring the boundaries of that capacity in his notion of conformity as it pertains to the epistemological structure of man, and in doing so, he identifies the various epistemological strands. For Charnock, these epistemological strands speak to the aspiring to the heights of knowledge of

---

and over the cattle, and over all the earth, and over every creeping thing that creepeth upon the earth. So God created man in his own image: in the image of God created he him: male and female created he them. And God blessed them, and God said unto them, Be fruitful and multiply, and replenish the earth, and subdue it: and have dominion over the fish of the sea, and over the fowl of the air, and over every living thing that moveth upon the earth. Col 3:10. And have put on the new man, which is renewed in knowledge, after the image of him that created him. Eph 4:24. And that ye put on the new man, which after God is created in righteousness and true holiness.

21. Charnock, "The Existence of God," in *Works*, 1:162.
22. Charnock, "A Discourse of the Knowledge of God," in *Works*, 4:29.
23. Charnock, "A Discourse of the Knowledge of God," in *Works*, 4:61.
24. Charnock, "A Discourse of the Knowledge of God," in *Works*, 4:61.

God that the creature is capable of in this temporal realm, which is consistent with the manifestation of the soul that has been regenerated in Christ through the Word and Spirit.

"Truth is the perfection of a rational understanding," Charnock reasons; therefore, "the highest truth must then be the highest perfection of it."[25] We find Charnock identifying the inherent capacity that God placed within the very design of man's mind and in doing so comes full circle with his notion of the soul's conformity to the imitable perfections of God. In the introduction, it was mentioned that Charnock in his *Discourse of the Knowledge of God* distills down an ultimate perspective of knowledge, the "sight of the beauty of God," which he identifies as "the end of the soul, and what is the end of a thing is the perfection of it."[26] Therefore, it is only natural in the soul's conformity to God's holiness that it would find its full capability merging from its very design. Conformity and capacity are joined together as the height of God's manifold grace in creating—better yet, resurrecting the soul in Christ. This, indeed, is the needle of grace embroidering, as well as hemming holiness in the soul.

Consequently, it presses the fullness of its capacity in the "sight of the beauty of God," which is the true "end of the soul."[27] This knowledge of God is, according to Charnock, the very purpose in God bringing forth creation, so that he could "communicate his goodness; the perfection of a soul, then, consists in the highest participation of that goodness according to its capacity."[28] Charnock elaborates on this conformity and capacity, which are identified in the epistemological strands and tethered in the image of God. According to Charnock,

> [t]he image of God consists in this knowledge, Col. 3:10. Every image is a participation of beams from the original. As darkness is the deformity of the world, and light the beauty of it, whereby the beauty of everything else is discovered, so knowledge is the beauty of the understanding, as ignorance is the deformity.[29]

---

25. Charnock, "A Discourse of the Knowledge of God," in *Works*, 4:94.

26. Charnock, "A Discourse of the Knowledge of God," in *Works*, 4:94.

27. Charnock, "A Discourse of the Knowledge of God," in *Works*, 4:94.

28. Charnock, "A Discourse of the Knowledge of God," in *Works*, 4:94. A recent discussion about the subject of participatory metaphysics as it relates to Stephen Charnock. See Michelson, "Reformed and Racially Orthodox?: Participatory Metaphysics, Reformed Scholasticism and Radical Orthodoxy's Critique of Modernity," 104–28.

29. Charnock, "A Discourse of the Knowledge of God," in *Works*, 4:94. The significance of this creaturely capacity is what Jonathan Edwards will attribute to the reality of

Furthermore, this illustrates the intrinsic nature of connectivity and the interrelatedness between conformity and deformity, as well as the epistemological relation and boundaries associated with the capacity which is intrinsically defined by that conformity or deformity. For example, Thomas Boston makes a note of the epistemological boundary; however, for him the Christian is to have an eye to that heavenly realm where the epistemological boundaries are redefined, because, for both Charnock and Boston, there is a more precise notion of God in heaven, that is, "a fuller perception of God."[30] For Boston, this "fuller perception of God," is indicative of the expansion of the epistemological capacity which awaits the child of God in heaven, and that epistemological construct is defined by two elements: intuitive and experimental knowledge. Boston notes, in extenuating this epistemological reality of the heavenly realm, that the full epistemological capacity awaits the child of God in heaven. According to Boston, "One may say, that the saints enjoy God and the Lamb in heaven, 1. By an intuitive knowledge; 2. By an experimental knowledge; both of them perfect." Moreover, what does he mean by the nature of this perfected knowledge that is defined as intuitive and experimental? "I mean," Boston maintains, "in respect of the capacity of the creature."[31] In what follows, Boston lays out the epistemological structure along with the epistemological trajectory concerning conformity and epistemological capacity in the temporal and eternal realm. He states:

---

eternal life and equates it to happiness, which he equates to the fullness of the capacity of the creature. "We are saved wholly and entirely by Christ's righteousness," says Edwards, "By salvation" is meant a perfect deliverance from all misery and the bestowment of eternal life; by "eternal life" is meant happiness that is perfect or that fills the capacity of the creature. See Edwards, "None Are Saved by Their Own Righteousness," in *Jonathan Edwards Sermons*.

30. Although the boundaries are redefined in some respect; however, this redefining does not change the epistemological limitations that are inherent within the creature. "In heaven," Charnock says, "God shall not be comprehensively known." It is true that "there will be a fuller perception of God, and a clearer notion of him in heaven; the infinite treasures of wisdom and goodness, which lie hid in God to be admired, will be then more clearly seen; yet God can never descend from his own infiniteness to be grasped by a created understanding. For in the highest pitch of glory, the soul is but finite, and therefore still too short to enclose an infinite being in its understanding, even to an endless eternity. In heaven, the glorified soul is still but a creature." See Charnock, "A Discourse of the Knowledge of God," in *Works*, 4:40.

31. Boston, "The Kingdom of Heaven" in *Works*, 8:332. Although Charnock does not say much about "intuitive" knowledge, other Puritans seem to identify this type of knowledge with that heavenly realm.

> The saints below enjoy God, in that knowledge they have of him by report, from his holy word, which they believe; they see him likewise darkly in the glass of ordinances, which do, as it were, represent the Bridegroom's picture, or shadow, while he is absent: they have also some experimental knowledge of him; they taste that God is good, and that the Lord is gracious. But the saints above shall not need a good report of the King, they shall see him; therefore faith ceaseth: they will behold his own face; therefore ordinances are no more: there is no need of a glass. They shall drink, and drink abundantly, of that whereof they have tasted; and so hope ceaseth, for they are at the utmost bounds of their desires.[32]

So, the nature of the content of the conception of God is defined by the nature of the soul being redeemed (i.e., regenerated) or not redeemed, and the epistemological boundaries are intrinsically defined according to conformity or deformity of that nature. Hence, we again find the notion of conformity bearing down upon the soul, and through this conformity, opening the soul's epistemological capacity to the extent possible in this temporal realm. Charnock explores this in his fourfold theory of knowledge.

i. Speculative Strand

This relational aspect of epistemology functions as a structure that manifests the dynamic nature of that relationship between God as the Creator or God as the Redeemer. It is the knowledge of the Redeemer, a saving knowledge, that Charnock sets out to distinguish, as well as establish the fullness of that redeeming knowledge ("properties of this knowledge") that defines the epistemological environment of the new creature. The inverse manifests itself as well, that is, there is speculative strand in our epistemological construct that is intrinsic to the soul that has been created in the image of God.

This speculative strand of knowledge is a natural knowledge or a "natural education," according to Charnock, "whereby they suck in and vent those notions rooted in them; in regard of natural principles in the soul, which conclude something about God, though nothing about Christ."[33] The reason for the break in this particular strand of knowledge is because this strand of knowledge is not "disposed for the perception of the object" (i.e., God).[34]

---

32. Boston, "The Kingdom of Heaven" in *Works*, 8:332.
33. Charnock, "A Discourse of the Knowledge of God," in *Works*, 4:16.
34. Charnock, "A Discourse of the Knowledge of God," in *Works*, 4:16.

Furthermore, this somewhat empty notion of knowledge, as far as it has no real tether point, is incapable of being a saving knowledge. At best this knowledge is a "foundation of a spiritual" knowledge; at worse, it is a justification for God's "proceedings in the hearts and consciences of the world"[35] by which the creature will be held accountable to the Creator.

The entirety of the epistemological construct must find itself within an environment that is not defined by a small capacity of man's ability to know or reason the things of God.[36] That is, the notion that bare reason is capable of penetrating the things of God has no possible foundation to build upon; it is incapable of bearing the weight of reality; more specifically, it cannot reach toward Christ. Instead, we find that the very idea of an untethered reason is an absurdity, according to Charnock, because mere reason, even in its "innocency was never a key fitted to all the wards of divine mysteries."[37] Not only are the "divine mysteries" beyond the reach of bare reason, bare reason, in and of itself, is plagued with several disabilities. Consider the following descriptors of reason that Charnock

---

35. Charnock, "A Discourse of the Knowledge of God," in *Works*, 4:17. According to Charnock, "it is the foundation of a spiritual: though a speculative might be without a spiritual, yet a spiritual cannot be without a speculative; a foundation may be without a superstructure, but a superstructure can never be without a foundation." Elsewhere Charnock says that "speculative knowledge is a sound of words and thoughts," lacking a "principle framed by a higher hand than that of nature." See Charnock, "A Discourse of the Knowledge of God," in *Works*, 4:16.

36. It has been demonstrated time and again that the even though the soul can reason; nonetheless, that capacity has been truncated or significantly impacted in its ability to function as it was intended to function, it is moving down a derailed track. Although the soul has been fitted by its Creator with the capacity to reason, that does not mean that capacity has become an ultimate autonomous discerner of reality or truth. So, if the height of reason's capacity had inherent limitations, before the Fall, it would seem all the more foolish to suggest that somehow the capacity to reason has a more discerning state in a deprived environment. Actually, unbridled reason produces the opposite result that it is seeking. "The knowledge we have by reason is uncertain," says Charnock, "because the mind of man is often prepossessed with crooked notions, which cannot be the rule to measure straight truths by." Despite this dim reality of reason, that is not the full depiction of its existence. Reason "is full of uncertainty, and dubious; and the more we know by natural reason, the more we doubt." See Charnock, "A Discourse of the Knowledge of God," in *Works*, 4:64. Edward Reynolds, "Heavenly things exceed the capacity of reason, for they are above what is called right reason; they contradict the wisdom of the flesh, for they are contrary to depraved reason: Nature stands in need of grace, for the right disposing of the mind to receive a supernatural object; and grace uses nature, that by strength of mind, clearness of judgment, and the light of good education, greater progress may be made in the study of the sacred writings." Reynold, *Animalis homo*.

37. Charnock, "A Discourse of the Knowledge of God in Christ," in *Works*, 4:154.

identifies the incompetency of reason: "blind in the things of God,"[38] it is "uncertain . . . a wandering vagabond, coins lies, and reports falsities as truths, an enemy to the knowledge of God in Christ."[39] Therefore, never "speak of right reason in the things of God," Charnock concludes, "without a supernatural illumination, and the guidance of revelation."[40] As a result, we are brought to the fact that our epistemological environment necessitates an intrinsic component or components that reason is incapable of providing; rather, as a result of the utmost "necessity of revelation and illumination"[41] reason is positioned, within this epistemological necessity, in a posture of submission to the divine authority of revelation.[42] Therefore, we should not take Charnock's position to be brutal with the intent to wipe away the faculty of reason because that is not the case. Instead, in the congruity of Charnock's thought with the Scriptures, he is looking to identify the faculty of reason as the Creator looks upon it. For example, "[t]he gospel doth not destroy reason and rational proceeding,"[43] Charnock affirms. Instead, "[i]t is agreeable to common reason, that old principles should be exploded, and appear unworthy, base, unreasonable, and weak, before new ones be introduced and entertained."[44]

This speculative, epistemological strand, for Charnock, speaks to the inescapable knowledge of God which functions as a reflective dome, that man finds himself both externally and internally encapsulated. That is, both externally and internally, no matter where man directs his attention, whether it is in the objective reality of creation or the subjective reality of the innermost recesses of his heart, he is exposed with the reflective light from the dome of God's creative work, which declares the reality

---

38. Charnock, "A Discourse of the Knowledge of God in Christ," in *Works*, 4:154.

39. Charnock, "A Discourse of the Knowledge of God in Christ," in *Works*, 4:156.

40. Charnock, "A Discourse of the Knowledge of God in Christ," in *Works*, 4:155. Charnock, throughout, makes clear that revelation is the fundamental structure of our knowing.

41. Charnock, "A Discourse of the Knowledge of God in Christ," in *Works*, 4:156.

42. Charnock, "A Discourse of the Knowledge of God in Christ," in *Works*, 4:157. Charnock notes: "We ought to submit our reason to revelation. God doth not give us reason to quarrel with, but to discern and entertain divine revelation. He hath given us reason to examine revelations, whether they bear a divine stamp upon them. He hath not therefore imposed things upon men without undeniable characters of their divine authority."

43. Charnock, "A Discourse of Conviction of Sin," in *Works*, 4:210.

44. Charnock, "A Discourse of Conviction of Sin," in *Works*, 4:210.

of God his Creator. Those who choose to suppress are still accountable, and the suppression does nothing more than increase their responsibility because they are covenantally bound to their Creator. Hence, the great divide that the framers of the Westminster Confession Faith speak of in 7:1. This covenantal aspect is stitched within the very fiber of their being since they have been created in this image of their Creator and the only way for man to escape such a reality is to move to the point of non-being; however, man can no more become non-being than he can become non-covenantal. This covenantal reality places man, always, within the ultimate environment of his Creator and makes him directly responsible to him. Therefore, it is one thing to know the nature of God, and another thing to know God in covenant as our God,[45] and that covenantal reality is a fundamental distinction, for Charnock, that exposes the vast chasm between "notional and fiducial knowledge."[46]

ii. Practical Strand

The substance behind Charnock's "another thing to know God in covenant as our God" is a functional transition point in his understanding of the two different epistemological strands of speculative and practical. In transitioning from the speculative strand to that of the practical strand, we find Charnock grounding it within the attributes of God. Charnock asserts,

> He is an object of faith as made known to us, but he is made known to us in some perfections of his nature, as encouragements to approach to him, and ground our hopes in him; and he is an object of faith in every one of his distinct attributes, in his power, wisdom, goodness, and righteousness . . . he is the object of faith as he is a God in covenant, our God; and he is our God in every attribute which makes up that glorious nature; and those perfections of his nature were made known in Christ, that he might be known not only speculatively, but fiducially.[47]

This fiducial aspect brings about and entwines the practical strand with the speculative strand, and the result is an epistemological capacity that did not exist before the object of faith being made known to the soul. That is, the speculative consists of only a "natural strength of

---

45. Charnock, "A Discourse of the Knowledge of God," in *Works*, 4:57.
46. Charnock, "A Discourse of the Knowledge of God," in *Works*, 4:59.
47. Charnock, "A Discourse of the Object of Faith," in *Works*, 5:151.

understanding," says Charnock; however, he notes in stark contrast that the practical knowledge "is the effect of an infused faith and the Spirit's operation."[48] However, although the two are distinct, the force of the one is found when it is bound to the other. For example, Charnock points out that "one knows God in the Scripture by reading [speculative strand]," yet, it is this speculative strand bound to the practical that allows one to know by a sense of relishing and "what he reads with his eye," Charnock notes, "is drawn by a divine pencil in the soul."[49]

In, *Conscience with the Power and Cases Thereof*, William Ames (1576–1633) under the section "Of Knowledge" asks: "What a man ought to doe that he may obtaine solid knowledge?" In response, he offers up ten different answers to this question of obtaining a solid knowledge which is contained with an emphasis on the practice of piety. In the first answer, he states that "the mind is wholly to be devoted unto piety" and closes with the tenth answer that "knowledge which we have obtained must be turn'd into use and practice."[50] It is this "turn'd into use and practice" that Charnock identifies as the core of the practical epistemological strand, and this core contains the covenantal reality of God in covenant. Accordingly, Charnock points out that

> [w]hen the knowledge of the nature of God is impressed upon us for imitation, and is, as the conference of Christ with his disciples, inflaming the heart, Luke 24:32, and driving away the cold affections towards God; when righteousness is understood as well as judgment, and that as a path, and a good path, to walk in; when we are not only directed to the path, but are pleased with the

---

48. Charnock, "A Discourse of the Knowledge of God," in *Works*, 4:20.

49. Charnock, "A Discourse of the Knowledge of God," in *Works*, 4:20.

50. The whole of this work has a great emphasis on the practice of piety. The influence of William Ames cannot be overstated, not just to those who were in close proximity to him in terms of time, but also those who were separated by hundreds of years. For example, it is suggested that Ames's *Conscience with the Power and Cases Thereof* was a filter that Edwards employed in his *Religious Affections* to decipher "individual experiences." As Ames informs us in the preface to that work, the plan of the book and the need for it were first suggested by the lectures of Perkins. It seemed to him that Protestant divines should have guidance in understanding and interpreting the experiences of their parishioners, especially where difficult cases of conscience and decision were involved. See Smith, "Editor's Introduction," in *Religious Affections*, ed. John E. Smith and Harry S. Stout, Revised edition., vol. 2, The Works of Jonathan Edwards, 68.

goodness of it, and the approving wisdom enters into the heart, and the knowledge of it becomes pleasant to the soul.[51]

This core covenantal element is expressed by Charnock "as the conference of Christ," which he identifies as the living component. This living component inflames the heart, which is a necessity, and without it we simply operate in an absurdity in our understanding of knowledge. This is because "it can no more rationally be called a knowledge of God," Charnock contends, "since it hath no life and soul in it, than a dead carcase can be called a man."[52] Furthermore, Charnock clarifies the distinction of the living component of this knowledge of God that is contained in the practical strand. He draws out this necessary epistemological distinction between the head and heart by noting that "thinking of God and Christ with the head, and embracing Christ with the heart, are two distinct things." It is "as the seeing a country in a map, and by travelling over it with our feet, are different kinds of knowledge." In Charnock's mind, this defining aspect of the practical strand is that it conforms with the "true end of knowledge," which is a knowledge that has descended into the practice of piety.[53] It is from this that he concludes that "one is a knowledge of the truth, the other 'an acknowledgment of it as it is after godliness,' Tit. 1:1."[54]

This passage from Titus is a foundational text that functions as an epicenter of what constitutes Christian theology, more specifically, the substance of that practical reality. "Christian theology," Mastricht submits, "unite[s] theory with practice," and is "a knowledge of the truth that is according to godliness (Titus 1:1)."[55] The practical unity points to the implementation of a heavenly reality in the temporal realm which, in some respect, is the sum and substance of the Puritans's notion of experimental knowledge, albeit connected here with the practical. Therefore, Mastricht speaking of the degrees of knowledge notes a qualitative difference in knowledge when we consider "a saving, experimental, practical knowledge that strives earnestly for the inner man so that from there it might bring forth the practical application of what is known."[56] The

---

51. Charnock, "A Discourse of the Knowledge of God," in *Works*, 4:18.
52. Charnock, "A Discourse of the Knowledge of God," in *Works*, 4:17.
53. Charnock, "A Discourse of the Knowledge of God," in *Works*, 4:16.
54. Charnock, "A Discourse of the Knowledge of God," in *Works*, 4:17.
55. Van Mastricht, *Theoretical and Practical Theology*, 1:78–79.
56. Van Mastricht, *Theoretical and Practical Theology*, 1:90. Scriptural references noted by Mastricht: John 13:17; Phil 3:8,10; 4:9; Col 1:9–10.

totality of this doctrine and knowledge which is the whole of theology is summed up, for Mastricht, in Titus 1:1 text, "in the words of the apostle, the "knowledge of the truth according to godliness."[57] This doctrine of knowledge is not a bare theory or something to be merely conjectured about; rather, it is the "power of godliness . . . since bare theory offers nothing but its form (2 Tim. 3:5)."[58] Therefore, the very nature of this practical theology should be accompanied by "an experimental study of theology," declares Mastricht, "in which we not only understand but also experience the force and efficacy of each theological head."[59]

The aforementioned practical epistemological content, expressed by Ames, in turning our knowledge into practice and Mastricht's identifying the necessity to understand, as well as experience "the force and efficacy of each theological head,"[60] finds a summative statement in Charnock, when he said that there needs to be a "knowledge of the object, and an embracing the end of that knowledge."[61] So, the "force and efficacy" is rooted in the covenantal reality, and this covenantal reality is the essential reality contained in a knowledge of the truth that accompanies godliness. This conjoining nature of knowledge of truth and godliness is expressed in Titus 1:1, which is identified by Charnock as an implicit reality of the "image of God engraven upon the heart," which speaks to "a heart to be his people, as God hath a heart to be our God."[62] This references the covenantal language of Jer 24:7, "I will give them an heart to know Me, that I am the Lord; and they shall be my people, and I will be their God, for they shall return to me with their whole heart." Charnock concludes that the "evangelical promise is not so much to give us an head (though that is included), as a heart to know God."[63]

---

57. Van Mastricht, *Theoretical and Practical Theology*, 1:90.

58. Van Mastricht, *Theoretical and Practical Theology*, 1:96.

59. Van Mastricht, *Theoretical and Practical Theology*, 1:97. On a couple of different occasions, Mastricht will employ this phraseology "force and efficacy" to underscore the significance of the power of godliness.

60. Van Mastricht, *Theoretical and Practical Theology*, 1:97.

61. Charnock, "A Discourse of the Knowledge of God," in *Works*, 4:17.

62. Charnock, "A Discourse of the Knowledge of God," in *Works*, 4:17.

63. Charnock, "A Discourse of the Knowledge of God," in *Works*, 4:17.

iii. Nexus of Speculative and Practical Strands

It is necessary to consider further the practical epistemological strand which comes to a fuller understanding when taken in conjunction with the speculative strand. Especially, the nexus that entwines them together which, for Charnock, speaks to the "necessity of revelation and illumination" that establishes the nexus between the two epistemological strands: speculative and practical.

According to Charnock, speculative knowledge is a natural knowledge or infused knowledge within the soul of man.[64] It is here that Charnock in a similar fashion as Calvin speaks of the *sensus deitatis*; however, he does not employ that particular phrase. Charnock uses another phrase, "impression of a deity,"[65] to express similar thoughts as Calvin about the *sensus deitatis*. He describes this "impression of a deity" as "a relic of knowledge after the fall of Adam," and it is like a fire that is kindling under the layer of ashes or "a notion sealed up in the soul of every man."[66] More specifically, according to Charnock, "the notion of God seems to be twisted with the nature of man, and is the first natural branch of common reason, or upon either the first inspection of a man into himself and his own estate and constitution, or upon the first sight of any external visible object."[67] He notes further that we "know nothing of God by the creatures," says Charnock, "but as God spreads an inward light upon the mind. In nature, there is a manifestation in us, as well as a manifestation to us, Rom. i.19, yet it is a common

---

64. Charnock, "A Discourse of the Knowledge of God," in *Works*, 4:17. This aspect of knowledge is impressive, could not the same be said for the regeneration of the soul? You cannot have regeneration without the spiritual; however, you can have a soul without the spiritual? Yet, a man in the nature of his soul has no 'real' foundation that his soul's superstructure is established upon until the Spirit of God infuses or implants that substratum that enlivens and infiltrates the faculties of the soul.

65. Charnock, "The Existence of God," in *Works*, 1:137.

66. Charnock, "The Existence of God," in *Works*, 1:137.

67. Charnock, "The Existence of God," in *Works*, 1:137. Although the language is different, there is a striking resemblance between Charnock and Calvin, especially in Calvin's *Institutes* dealing with the knowledge of God. Charnock continues, "Nature within man, and nature without man, agree upon the first meeting together to form this sentiment, that there is a God. It is as natural as anything we call a common principle ... so that this truth is as natural to man as anything he can call most natural or a common principle." He emphasizes the nature of the impression being twisted into the nature of man by noting that it is so deeply embedded within man, and it cannot be rooted out, nor can it "be struck out by the malice and power of hell."

A SOUL FRAMED IN CHRIST

illumination"[68]—consequently, the reason that "there is a necessity of revelation and illumination."[69]

Charnock offers these sub-divisions for his previous divisions of knowledge (speculative, practical, experiential, interest).[70] Alternatively, perhaps, they are foundational blocks to be added to the speculative as a man is transformed from the state of depravity to the state of grace. "There must be," Charnock asserts, "first an external revelation of the object; secondly, an internal illumination of the faculty. There is a word of revelation, which is the gospel revealed to the understandings of men; there is a Spirit of revelation requisite besides."[71] Although there appears, at first, to be similarities to the categories mentioned above, these words of Charnock seem to suggest something more. At least there is something between the point of unregenerate and regenerate state that takes place; the necessity of revelation and illumination defines that. In this case, there is a different aspect of knowledge, and it would emerge as a subset between the speculative strand of knowledge that is "in the bark of the letter, not in the sap of the Spirit,"[72] which cannot lead to regeneration. There is a practical strand, which "is an enlivening knowledge and a likening knowledge"[73] that is characteristic of the heart being inflamed, which appears to be after regeneration.

If the speculative strand is not capable of leading to salvation and the practical strand is the knowledge sinking into the soul, where is the "necessity of revelation and illumination" to fit within the confines of Charnock's knowledge? We should not misunderstand Charnock's purpose in these distinctions; the speculative is a crucial epistemological strand of knowledge; however, it is not to be "bare speculation." It is "not in a bare speculation, without engaging our affections, and making every notion of the divine eternity end in a suitable impression upon our hearts. If so, it would be much like the disciples gazing upon the heavens at the ascension of their Master, while they forget the practice of his orders, Acts 1:11. We may else find something

68. Charnock, "The Knowledge of God in Christ," in *Works*, 4:155–56.

69. Charnock, "The Knowledge of God in Christ," in *Works*, 4:155–56.

70. There is a need for additional research with Charnock's divisions of knowledge. Is this something that Charnock is pulling out of Aristotle's *De Anima* or Aquinas commentary on *De Anima*? Aristotle does make such distinctions about speculative, practical, and appetition in *De Anima* 433a14–26; 820–25.

71. Charnock, "The Knowledge of God in Christ," in *Works*, 4:157.

72. Charnock, "A Discourse of the Knowledge of God," in *Works*, 4:16.

73. Charnock, "A Discourse of the Knowledge of God," in *Works*, 4:18.

of the nature of God, and lose ourselves, not only in eternity, but to eternity."[74] How is one transported from the speculative, or how is it that there is a superstructure built on the speculative in order to arrive in the realm of practical knowledge? Better yet how is it that speculative and practical become intertwined to the benefit of the redeemed soul?

Charnock, speaks of a "spiritual knowledge" that is, to some degree of the "practical," perhaps, the incipient or subset of the "practical knowledge." However, when Charnock speaks of spiritual knowledge it is within the context of practical knowledge, because there is an interconnectedness in Charnock's thought between the inner nature of man and his outward conduct, more specifically, "spiritual knowledge is always attended with a spiritual life."[75] Is this to suggest that it is impossible to separate the true theology from piety? So, it would appear that this connective tissue is spiritual illumination that brings the two together; it is the transporting mechanism from speculative knowledge to practical knowledge, in Charnock's concept of spiritual illumination. Charnock makes the following remark about illumination, "but God, being infinitely perfect, 'works all things in all' immediately, 1 Cor. xii. 6. Illumination, sanctification, grace, &c., are the immediate works of God in the heart."[76] It is here that

---

74. Charnock, "A Discourse upon the Eternity of God," in *Works* 1:372–73. Elsewhere, Charnock will label this kind of reality in the soul as an "evangelical impression." See Charnock, "The Necessity of Regeneration," in *Works*, 3:29. Charnock asks: "What evangelical duties can be performed without an evangelical impression, without the forming of Christ and the doctrine of Christ in the heart, not only in the notion, but the operative and penetrating power of it?" Here we see the notion of conformity in Charnock's thought being expressed by "evangelical impression." In this instance we find the full substance that Charnock has placed within this notion of "evangelical impression," that is, it has a forming factor in the heart that stands in relation to the real holiness associated with regeneration. The aforementioned is the content of this expression, and a little later in the same discourse, we find Charnock expressing the weight of the reality contained in "evangelical impression," 3:29. For example, "An evangelical head," says Charnock, "will be but drier fuel for eternal burning, without an evangelical impression upon the heart and the badge of a new nature," 3:59. The intensity of this reality is stepped up, by Charnock, in the last two times he uses "evangelical impression"; it is done with an absolute nature of the state of man in or out of Christ. He asked: "Where is the evangelical impression upon your soul?" 3:65. Moreover, in this last use, he offers to opposite absolute reality, "The new creation is an evangelical impression, and therefore corresponds in its intention with the gospel," 3:100.

75. Charnock, "A Discourse in the Knowledge of God," in *Works* 4:18.

76. Charnock, "The Existence of God," in *Works*, 1:437. See Charnock, "The Efficient of Regeneration," in *Works*, 3:253 and Charnock, "God the Author of Reconciliation," in *Works*, 3:440. First, Charnock speaking of mystery notes, "As it had God for

Charnock employs similar language that is characteristic of God's manner of regeneration; that is, something that did not exist comes into existence by the sovereign work of God's Spirit. Furthermore, Charnock points out that "the frame of grace is raised upon the infused notions of God; illumination precedes renovation of the will."[77] It is here that we have, to an extent, come full circle with Charnock's philosophy of regeneration and find the epistemological strands rooted and tethered in the reality of regeneration. Here again is his definition of regeneration:

> A supernatural renewing grace, must expel corrupt habits from the will, and reduce it to its true object. When faith is planted, it brings love to work by: when the soul is renewed, there is an harmony between God and the heart, between the mind and the word, between the will and the duty: when the appetite, and true taste of the soul, is restored in regeneration, then spring up strong desires to apply itself to every holy service.[78]

So, not only does this speak to a necessity in regeneration, but this also suggests that there is a fundamental link between speculative and practical knowledge, that is "spiritual illuminations."[79] Speaking of the knowledge of God, Charnock states:

---

the author, so we must have God for the teacher of it; the contrivance was his, and the illumination of our minds must be from him. As God only manifested the gospel, so he only can open our eyes to the mysteries of Christ in it." Here Charnock speaking of conversion states, "The work is therefore called creation, a resurrection, to shew its irresistible power; it is called illumination, persuasion, drawing, to shew the suitableness of its efficacy to the nature of the human faculties." Charnock, "The Knowledge of God," in *Works*, 4:73. "We are no more born with a saving knowledge of God in our heads and hearts, than with a skill in philosophy and mathematics; no, nor so much, for we bring into the world a faculty capable of them by ordinary instruction, but uncapable of the other without special illumination." Charnock, "The Knowledge of God," in *Works*, 4:102. "Since our understanding is corrupted by sin, and filled with error, it is not sufficient to understand the things of God without an internal illumination, as well as an external revelation." Charnock, "The Knowledge of God," in *Works*, 4:11. "And whatsoever saving knowledge any man hath of God, is by the special illumination of this true light by the virtue of his Spirit."

77. Charnock, "A Discourse of the Knowledge of God," in *Works*, 4:35, 70. A little further down, Charnock makes clear the significance and connection with "illumination." He notes, "We see here the order of God's working, if knowledge be a necessary means. First knowledge, then grace; first knowledge, then that life which is eternal. No house can possibly be built without a foundation; the groundwork first, then the superstructure. Illumination leads the way, and the inclinations of the will follow."

78. Charnock, *The Doctrine of Regeneration*, 46–47.

79. Charnock, "A Discourse of the Knowledge of God," in *Works*, 4:25. It is important

> This is a knowledge above the knowledge of nature; that is too muddy to be a spring of any spiritual action, raised above or hearty reliance. It is not a knowledge of God by rational deductions, but spiritual illuminations. The knowledge of God in the creatures is as the dawn; the knowledge of God in the Scripture is as the day-spring. But what is either dawn or day-spring to a blind eye? The day-spring may be in the world, yet not in our hearts; we cannot work without light, and though there be the greatest light, we cannot work without sight.[80]

God's manner of regeneration does, indeed, deal with the whole of man and not just a particular aspect of his life, of his will, of his affections; instead, the totality of man is rolled up into the magnificent redemptive work of Christ. It is in this redemptive work that shadows are replaced with the realty, and the "day-spring" comes in to clear view because this there has to be real content, spiritual knowledge, that accompanies that "the knowledge of Scripture itself."[81] This fact is easily demonstrated about the great Sanhedrim, Nicodemus, who understood the letter of the Scripture, yet to what advantage was this knowledge for Nicodemus? In Charnock's estimation, it was an untethered knowledge, a speculative knowledge with no grounding. That is, an "evangelical head" that will only serve to fuel the "eternal burning, without an evangelical impression upon the heart and the badge of a new nature."[82]

Therefore, the entirety of this entwining of the speculative and practical strands is the manifestation of an "evangelical impression" upon the epistemological construct of a soul that has been redeemed in Christ. Saving knowledge is a multifaceted epistemological construct which consists of, at least, speculative, and practical; however, Charnock seems to suggest that any Christian that is satisfied with the speculative and practical finds themselves lacking other crucial components to that epistemological

---

to specify this as "spiritual illumination," especially for Charnock, because he also speaks of "common illumination." "The true nature of saving illumination consists in this," says Owen, "that it gives the mind such a direct intuitive insight and prospect into spiritual things as that, in their own spiritual nature, they suit, please, and satisfy it, so that it is transformed into them, cast into the mould of them, and rests in them." See Owen, "Works of the Holy Spirit Preparatory unto Regeneration," in *Works*, 3:238.

80. Charnock, "A Discourse of the Knowledge of God," in *Works*, 4:25.
81. Charnock, "The Necessity of Regeneration," in *Works*, 3:59.
82. Charnock, "The Necessity of Regeneration," in *Works*, 3:59.

construct. Subsequently, this brings us to the third epistemological strand of Charnock's theory of knowledge—experiential knowledge.[83]

iv. Experiential Strand

The experiential strand of Charnock's epistemology is interesting because, on the surface, it would seem that it is another way of identifying the practical strand of epistemology. What is the difference between a practical and experiential type of knowledge? Don't they both entail the living out the personal convictions in life and experience or seeking to experience the spiritual truths in living out that truth? Why does Charnock not just identify the necessity of the practical aspect of knowledge and identify within the practical aspect of knowledge an experiential facet of that practical knowledge? Furthermore, what benefit is there in further segmenting this type of knowledge from the practical? That is, if the two types of knowledge are so tightly defined, what significance can there be in identifying this particular epistemological strand in Charnock's theory of knowledge?

The functionality of Charnock's experiential knowledge is multifold in his system of thought. Not only is it comprehensive in the life of a Christian, but it is just as deep—if not more so—in its grounding nature for the believer, that is, a comforting aspect of the practical knowledge. This is the reason for the various epistemological strands. In Charnock's mind, each strand is being bound or twisted together, furthering the depth, width, and height of the sight of God that will be fully manifested in the heavenly realm when we know as we are known. So, the experiential is that portion of knowledge that allows the believer to taste an aspect of that heavenly realm before arriving in that realm.

For Charnock, this experiential[84] aspect of knowledge functions as ballast to stabilize the soul in the sense that it further solidifies the knowledge

---

83. Although the experiential aspect of knowledge is of great significance for the Puritans, they were not the only ones who identified the significance of it. There is a clear lineage of the importance of the experiential aspect of knowledge identified in St. Augustine, St. Bernard of Clairvaux, St. Aquinas, Martin Luther, and Calvin. See Geybels, *Cognitio Dei Experimentalis: A Theological Genealogy of Christian Religious Experience*. Hordern, *Experience and Faith: The Significance of Luther for Understanding Today's Experiential Religion*. For experimental knowledge in the works of Aquinas, see Dedek, *Experimental Knowledge of Indwelling Trinity: An Historical Study of the Doctrine of St. Thomas*.

84. Charnock will note that the experiential is not a necessity of saving knowledge;

of the child of God in tasting and seeing that the Lord is good. However, the other ballast aspect of this experiential knowledge is the solidification of the glorious truth of the gospel reality found in the mediating work of Christ. This experimental aspect is a settling factor of the truth found in Christ being our high priest; more specifically, it was a necessity for the qualification of his compassion toward us. So, not only does he relate, but he relates experimentally, and this reality has a reverberating impact on a soul that is renewed in Christ that brings about comfort and peace unknown to those who are alienated from the Creator.

Also, as mentioned earlier, there is a bonding component to the experiential nature of knowledge that cannot be identified with the other aspects of knowing (speculative and practical), for Charnock. In Charnock's mind, the experiential component serves to heighten and deepen

---

however, in doing so, he does emphasize that experiential, along with interest, are "necessary to the comfort of knowledge," as well as to our well-being as a Christians. This being the case, one could easily undermine the experiential type of knowledge. It will seem, to some extent, that this experiential, as a comforting aspect, is not as important as the other types of knowledge. If that is the case, we would need to ask what is the significance of comfort in knowledge is? Is it just in experiential knowledge that comfort plays a part? Yet, this facet of comfort is more than surface level, because comfort is something Charnock will attribute to the degree of understanding, for example, as "the operations of the will depend upon the touch of the understanding, so the comforts of the soul depend upon the clearness of the understanding contemplating the object." See Charnock, "A Discourse of the Knowledge of God," in *Works*, 4:37. There is, yet another linking element that conjoins the whole of the epistemological construct together, not just the four strands but internal functionality that causes for a holistic understanding. Instead, there is a direct correlation between comfort and understanding, if the soul's comfort is directly tethered to the "clearness of the understanding" in its "contemplating the object," then this experiential epistemological strand is an addition to that "clearness of the understanding" and contributes to the reality of this comfort. See Charnock, "A Discourse of the Knowledge of God," in *Works*, 4:22. However, other men, such as Thomas Brooks and Thomas Boston, place a greater emphasis on experiential knowledge and place it within the confines of a necessity of saving knowledge. For example, "The apostle well know that all notional and speculative knowledge would leave men on this side [of] heaven, and therefore he earnestly prays that their knowledge might be experimental, that being the knowledge that accompanies salvation, that will give a man at last possession of salvation." See Brooks, *The Complete Works of Thomas Brooks*, 2:436. Boston speaks more directly, "If you have not the experimental knowledge of Christ," says Boston, "all your knowledge is in vain as to the salvation of your soul." See Boston, "A Discourse on the Experimental Knowledge of Christ," in *Works*, 2:645. Sibbes "I add, because we shall experimentally feel the life of Christ manifested to us. It is that that makes a Christian. Experience is the life [of] a Christian. What is all knowledge of Christ without experience, but a bare knowledge, if the power that raised Christ's body raise not our souls?" See Sibbes, *The Complete Works of Richard Sibbes*, 4:412.

the magnitude of our spiritual understanding, as well as congeal the other components of knowledge, and more so our spiritual understanding of the work of Christ. This experiential aspect pulls back the cover of Christ's works and allows us to get a sense, in addition to our understanding and to the best of our capacity, of what Christ did for us. "The understanding is," Charnock maintains, "but the door of the heart; to let God and Christ stick there, and not bring them into the heart, is to give a cold entertainment to that which deserves the best." Furthermore, it intensified the qualification of the compassion of Christ's work. "Qualification of compassion," Charnock notes, "could not result in such a manner from anything so well as from an experimental knowledge of the miseries he had contracted; and this must be by a sense and feeling of them."[85] The substance of reality that is contained in this aspect of experiential knowledge—"experimental knowledge of the miseries he [Christ] had contracted"—should not be dismissed or devalued. Perhaps, we find Charnock echoing the thoughts of William Perkins (1558–1602).[86]

The substance of this knowledge would be what Perkins would identify as the very core of experiential knowledge, and he speaks of it with a degree of intensity. For example, Perkins in his *A Declaration of the True Manner of Knowing Christ Crucified* emphatically points out[87] that there is to be a depth of experiential knowledge "because we ought to have experience of it [Christ's resurrection], in our hearts and lives."[88] Furthermore,

---

85. Charnock, "A Discourse of the Necessity of Christ's Death," in *Works* 5:36.

86. The influence and connection of thought between William Perkins and Stephen Charnock have been researched and detailed in a dissertation by Hansang Lee. See Lee, "Trinitarian Theology and Piety: The Attributes of God in the Thought of Stephen Charnock (1628–1680) and William Perkins (1558–1602)."

87. By emphatic, I mean that he employs strong language repeatedly ("should labour by all means possible to feele the power of Christs death killing and mortifying our sinnes." See Perkins, *A Declaration of the True Manner of Knowing Christ Crucified*, 821.

88. Perkins, *A Declaration of the True Manner of Knowing Christ Crucified*, 821. There is another facet to this notion of depth as it pertains to the experiential knowledge—'sense of.' Charnock will often make references to the "sense of" and does mention on a few occasions "knowledge and sense of." John Owen notes the importance of this sense; however, he does so in order to make the distinction between faith and this "sense of" and demonstrates that the former is more important than the latter. Regardless, there seems to be a depth added to our understanding when the understanding is entwined with a 'sense of' what is understood, hence, the "knowledge and sense" is something that Charnock points out in our knowledge of God. This notion of having a "sense of" is deeply rooted in the Puritans' understanding of a knowledge of God and it is something that Jonathan Edwards will make a vital component of his understanding of who God is

Perkins states that this experience should be accompanied with a laboring that we might feel the power of Christ's death and all that is contained in that reality, "We should labour," Perkins declares, "by all meanes possible to feele the power of Christ's death killing and mortifying our sinnes . . . labour by experience to see and feele the very death of it [sin], and to lay it as it were in a grave never to rise againe."[89]

Not only does Perkins speak with intensity about the experiential knowledge or what Perkins often calls a "feeling knowledge," which he uses as a bonding agent, so to speak, as Charnock's experiential knowledge that produces certainty. The "knowledge of the elect," Perkins says, "is pure, certain, sure, distinct, and particular: for it is joined with a feeling and inward experience of the thing known."[90] So, in light of Perkins's perspective of this "feeling knowledge," we find Charnock, not only in agreement but echoing the thoughts of Perkins when addressing the nature of certainty as it pertains this type of knowledge and its ability to bind together, with a substantive reality, speculative and practical knowledge.[91]

For Charnock, the answer to the proximity of these two types of knowledge—practical and experiential—is, for Charnock, another fiber to be entwined to the totality of our epistemological construct with the trajectory directly related to the heavenly realm. That is, the soul was fashioned with an "experimental sense," which is expressed in a phrase attributed to Junius, that is, *gustus spiritualis judicii* defined as "a witness of the truth in us, 1 John v.10."[92]

---

toward a redeemed soul and the apprehension of the beauty of holiness. See Stein, "The Quest for the Spiritual Sense: The Biblical Hermeneutics of Jonathan Edwards," 99–113. See Miller, "Jonathan Edwards on the Sense of the Heart," 123–45. See Erdt, *Jonathan Edwards, Art and the Sense of the Heart*. Brad Walton, in his thesis, draws out this notion of "knowledge and sense" as it pertains to the Puritans leading up to Edwards's "sense of heart." Walton references Charnock several times in his understanding of the "heart" in this context. See Walton, "'Formerly Approved and Applauded' The Continuity of Edwards's Treatise Concerning Religious Affections with Seventeenth-Century Puritan Analyses of True Piety, Spiritual Sensation and Heart-Religion," 258–318.

89. Perkins, *A Declaration of the True Manner of Knowing Christ Crucified*, 822.

90. Perkins, *The Estate of a Christian in this Life*, 587.

91. Perkins, *A Declaration of the True Manner of Knowing Christ Crucified*, 821. Charnock does what Perkins has done throughout his works, anchored this reality in the notion of conformity, more specifically, "confomoritie with Christ," Perkins says, "standes either in the framing of our inward and spirituall life, in in the practice of outward and morall duties."

92. Charnock, "A Discourse of the Knowledge of God," in *Works*, 4:19. Edward Reynolds (1599–1676) attributes this phrase to Junius as well. Although neither man

The substance found in this expression is directed at the spiritual sense of knowledge that is accompanied by a discernment in such a way that it could be suggested that this *gustus spiritualis judicii* is the manifestation of a mature experiential knowledge "which is not only knowledge by the understanding," Charnock contends, "but a knowledge by a spiritual sense."[93] There is a restorative aspect of the image contained in this notion of *gustus spiritualis judicii*; this would seem to be the case in Junius's understanding because one of the consequences of sin was "the perversion of our judgment," he says, "with the sediment of our senses, so to speak, removing

---

identifies where it is that Junius uses this phrase, Reynolds does note that "Junius somewhere calls it a "spiritual taste of judgement." Reynolds states, "quod franciscus junius alicubi vocat 'gustum spiritualis judicii,' quo quis sanam ac caelestem doctrinam a fermentio et insipidis ineptiis discernit, et solius 'Christi vocem audit,' et agnoscit." This Latin expression *"gustus spiritualis judicii"* is used by the following Puritans: Stephen Charnock, John Flavel, and Edward Reynolds. The source of Charnock's use is in reference to Franciscus Junius; however, there is no text reference. Reynolds in his sermon *Animalis Homo;* see Reynolds, 374 "Proinde 4. discant oves Christi ea, quae de Deo et Christo in Evangelii praedicatione tradita sunt, pro modo et mensura spiritualis judicii "probare, et quae bona sunt," uti docet Apostolus, "fide retinere." Reynolds identifies the substance of this phrase in Paul's words in 1 Thess 5:21, "Prove all things, hold fast that which is good." Reynolds, a little further down, in this sermon, gives another sense of this phrase. Reynolds asserts, "Continuis previbus et assidua communione Spiritus Sancti conservandus est his spiritualis judicii gustus: iis enim qui secundum pietatis norman vitam componunt, doctrinam suam Christus patefacere promisit." Here there is an aspect of the Holy Spirit preserving this spiritual sense, especially in our communion with the Holy Spirit, which is in accordance with a life of piety. Earlier in this sermon, he speaks of the relationship between God's revelation, the work of the grace of Christ and the Spirit of God which effectively opens and softens the heart that is may proportionately know the sweetness of the spiritual truth in Christ. In Reynolds words: "Ex quibis ita explicatis, manifeste sequitur, ad perfectam et propriam rerum supernaturalium cognitionem, non sufficere ex parte objecti Revelationem, nec ex parte subjecti debitum usum rectae rationis; sed insuper requiri Gratiam Christi et speciale adjutorium Spiritus Sancti, quo cor aperiatur, emolliatur, et supernaturalis veritatis dulcedini habeat proportionatam et gustum spiritualis judicii." 368. See Goodwin, *The Works of Thomas Goodwin*, 1: xxix. This content encompassed within this phrase was attributed to Thomas Goodwin, "This light was attended, so far as we can judge, with an inward sense of spiritual things, with a *gustus spiritualis judicii*, which, after long experience, grew up into senses exercised to discern good and evil, and into an abounding in all knowledge and sense. And, indeed, that person is the best interpreter, who (besides other helps) hath a comment in his own heart; and he best interprets Paul's Epistles, who is himself the epistle of Christ written by the Spirit of God. He best understands Paul's Epistles, who hath Paul's sense, temptations, and experience."

93. Charnock, "A Discourse of the Knowledge of God," in *Works*, 4:19. "It is an affective knowledge. All saving knowledge," says Charnock, "is full of sense." See Charnock, "A Discourse of the Knowledge of God," in *Works*, 4:44.

spiritual tastes from our minds."⁹⁴ Therefore, according to Flavel, the reality expressed in this notion of *gustus spiritualis judicii* is indeed a spiritual sense or taste that is restored in conjunction with the principle of holiness. That is, "a spiritual taste, by which those that have their senses exercised," Flavel notes, "can distinguish things that differ. "The spiritual man judgeth all things" (1 Cor 2:15). "His ear tries words, as his mouth tasteth meats" (Job 34:3). Swallow nothing (let it come never so speciously) that hath not some relish of Christ and holiness in it."⁹⁵

So, to a certain extent, for Charnock, this *gustus spiritualis judicii* is an intrinsic functionality of this experimental knowledge. And his understanding of αἴσθησις found in Phil 1:9 clearly suggests that the experiential aspect contains a full realm of reality to be perceived or has the capacity to perceive and understand.⁹⁶ That experiential sense offered up by Charnock echoes the thoughts of Perkins. Charnock avers:

> Labour to have the savour of truth upon your spirits, as well as the notions of it in your heads. The kingdom of God consists not in word, but in power; the new birth consists not in a bare notion, but in spiritual savour. The highest notional knowledge comes far short of experimental; the knowledge a blind man hath of light and colours, by hearing a lecture upon it, is but mere ignorance to the knowledge he would have if his eyes were opened. Endeavour to have the savour of Christ's ointments, Cant. 1:3, and inward sense exercised, Heb. 5:14. The apostle distinguisheth knowledge and judgment, Philip. 1:9. Knowledge is a notion in the head, judgment, or αἴσθησις, is the sense or savour of it in the heart.⁹⁷

---

94. Junius, *A Treatise on True Theology*, 95.

95. Flavel, "The Fountain Life Opened," in *Works*, 1:128.

96. How quickly we find the intertwinement of Charnock's epistemology consistently bound together. Here again, the relational reality of conformity and capacity are the bedrock of this knowledge in Christ.

97. Charnock, "A Discourse of the Word, The Instrument of Regeneration," in *Works* 3:334. We find similar words expressed by John Owen, "He gives αἴσθησιν πνευματικήν, a spiritual sense, a taste of the things themselves upon the mind, heart, and conscience; when we have αἰσθητήρια γεγυμνασμένα, 'senses exercised' to discern such things." See Owen, "Of The Divine Original Authority, Self-Evidencing Light, and Power, *in Works*, 16:327. See Louw and Nida, *Greek-English Lexicon of the New Testament: Based on Semantic Domains*, 383. Thomas Goodwin echoes this same emphasis, "And therefore in that 1 Cor. 2:9, the things of the gospel are called things 'prepared for them that love him'; they are suited, suited on purpose as it were to them; and in Philip. 1:9, the knowledge of the saints it is called sense ... We translate it 'in all judgment,' but it is a judgment which ariseth from, or at least is joined with sense, a taste, a suitableness that the soul hath to

Charnock finds a high degree of vitality in the reality contained in αἴσθησις, which is indicative of a spiritual sense or an experiential knowledge that functions as a solidifying component to our saving knowledge of Christ.[98] The nature of this reality is captured in the fact that experience, by design, according to Thomas Manton, "giveth us greater excitement to the love of Christ and his ways, for though love be built upon the proper reasons of love, yet it is increased by experience."[99] However, Manton points out that not only does experience increase our love for Christ, the experience is an agent of force, that is, the "proper reasons of love are necessity, excellency, and propriety, yet experience addeth a force to all these."[100] The idea of the "inward sense exercised" is insightful to the defining properties of this experiential strand because this is an instrument, for Charnock, to conjoin this aspect of "inward sense exercised" with the actuating of the same.

In *A Discourse Proving Weak Grace Victorious,* Charnock identifies another facet of this experiential knowledge that calls for actuation of that spiritual knowledge. What we find is the merging or unifying of the various faculties of man by demonstrating the internal relation between the understanding, will, and experience.[101] He continues to note that we need to

> [g]et a stock of spiritual knowledge, and actuate it often . . . Men whose religion consists rather in a commotion of their passions than a judicious and considerate determination of their wills . . . get the experience of every truth you hear. Experimental knowledge is the true ballast (stability) of the soul . . . an experimental

---

the things revealed." See Goodwin, *The Works of Thomas Goodwin,* 4:305–6.

98. Charnock, "A Discourse of the Word, The Instrument of Regeneration," in *Works* 3:334. Charnock's epistemology is consistently bound together; here again, the relational reality of conformity and capacity are the bedrock of this knowledge in Christ. It is in the new birth that there is a transition from that which lacks substance to that which is filled with experiential substance. This is the case because this experimental strand is not "a bare notion, but a spiritual savour"; this experiential knowledge is not a diminished notional aspect of knowledge; it is not disproportionate spiritual knowledge; rather, it is a knowledge defined by a spiritual taste, an "inward sense exercised."

99. Manton, *The Complete Works of Thomas Manton,* 20:53.

100. Manton, *The Complete Works of Thomas Manton,* 20:5.

101. There is an interesting connection or parallel of thought between what Charnock is expressing here and what would become a fundamental component of Jonathan Edwards's thought in his *Religious Affections,* more specifically, the development of this relational reality found in the faculties: will, understanding, and experience. See Edwards, *Religious Affections,* in *Works,* 2:272.

taste of the grace of God . . . It must be a taste, not only the hearing of a sound; it is not enough to be sound in judgment, but spiritual in taste, Col. 1:23.[102]

In this process of actuating knowledge is contained the gripping aspect of experimental knowledge that parallels the passage mentioned above. Except here we see the force of this experiential strand amplified, especially, when Charnock challenges us to "get the experience of every truth you hear . . . It must be a taste, not only the hearing of a sound."[103] Not only is this strand a bonding agent for the other epistemological strands, but it also functions as a stabilizer for the soul, a stability factor because, "[e]xperimental knowledge is the true ballast of the soul,"[104] declares Charnock.

v. Interest Strand

We should recall that Charnock has four epistemological strands: speculative, practical, experiential, and the fourth epistemological strand is knowledge of interest. In reference to the interest strand of knowledge, he notes that it sweetens "our imperfect happiness in this world . . . [and is] the foretaste of happiness."[105] It is the strand of interest that is associated with, at the end of this epistemological construct, a redeemed soul in this temporal realm. A soul which is able to transition from a mere glimpse of who God is in Christ as its Redeemer to getting a "clear sight of God[106] as the supreme good, the understanding is satisfied, the will filled with love, and all the desires of the soul find the centre of their rest."[107] It is the center of rest because the "happiness of heaven," asserts Charnock, is "the ultimate and complete happiness of the soul, which consists in a knowledge of God."[108] This is Charnock's

---

102. Charnock, "A Discourse Proving Weak Grace Victorious," in *Works* 5:281–82.
103. Charnock, "A Discourse Proving Weak Grace Victorious," in *Works* 5:224.
104. Charnock, "A Discourse Proving Weak Grace Victorious," in *Works* 5:281.
105. Charnock, "A Discourse of the Knowledge of God," in *Works* 4:22.
106. This "sight of God" is a phrase employed throughout Charnock's works; he uses this phrase some 43 times. This concept of gaining a "sight of God" is something that Jonathan Edwards will develop in great detail in what I perceive to be a fundamental aspect of his philosophical and theological works—pulling that reality of eternity into the temporal realm, so that the heavenly realm will not be surprising but all the more sweeter.
107. Charnock, "A Discourse of the Knowledge of God," in *Works*, 4:14.
108. Charnock, "A Discourse of the Knowledge of God," in *Works*, 4:24.

understanding of the fourth epistemological strand—knowledge of interest. Although one could question that since this ultimate aspect of knowledge is to be obtained in heaven, why the concern here on earth? This knowledge of interest is one of the many facets of Puritan theology that excels in their wanting to know, intimately, the God of heaven here in the temporal realm to the fullest extent possible. Therefore, concludes Charnock, "[t]he vision of God in heaven is the satisfaction of the soul, and the imperfect knowledge of him here is our imperfect felicity."[109]

It was this vision of God that was stripped from man the moment he entered into his fallen state, so the loss of this vision of God was the result of his depravity, and the defining ignorance in deformity.[110] It is for this reason that Charnock will connect this epistemological strand of interest directly with the redemptive work in the soul, because "there must be a renewing of his image before there be a vision of his face."[111] In addition, "[i]t is comfort upon this account, if new-born to heaven," Charnock reasons, "then to all things which may further your passage thither and assist you in it."[112] It is from this that Charnock associates that whole internal framework of our covenantally defined environment both to the conformity and capacity which is contained when we know God as Creator and Redeemer. The comprehensiveness of Charnock's understanding of this glorious relational reality, and the passage from the temporal to that heavenly realm, depicts the crowning aspect to our epistemological capacity that has been brought about in the conformity to the imitable perfections of God. Charnock articulates this comprehensive nature in the following:

> To God . . . to a sanctification of all states for a furtherance of you in your travel to and fitness for this kingdom; to a sight of God in his ordinances, and in his providences; he will not deny a beam here in his institutions to those for whom he reserves his full face

---

109. Charnock, "A Discourse of the Knowledge of God," in *Works*, 4:14. It is important to recall that for Charnock the sight or perfect sight is anchored in the end for which the sight was given: "The sight of the beauty of God is the end of the soul, and what is the end of a thing is the perfection of it." See Charnock, "The Knowledge of God," in *Works*, 4:94. Throughout Charnock's Discourses, we find the influence of Aristotle. See "ETHICA EUDEMIA," in *The Works of Aristotle*, vol. 9. See Flavel, "What is the life of glory but the vision of God, and the soul's assimilation to God by that vision?" in *Works* 2:95.

110. Charnock, "A Discourse upon God's Dominion," in *Works* 2:410.

111. Charnock, "A Discourse Upon the Holiness of God," in *Works*, 2:187. I think that we find the source of Boston's epistemological trajectory rooted in Charnock's epistemological strand of interest.

112. Charnock, "The Necessity of Regeneration," in *Works*, 3:66.

hereafter; to a fellowship with God in duties of worship, as a foretaste of a perpetual communion with him; to an improvement of all graces; to the perfectest dress at last of all beautiful grace, which may completely fit you for an everlasting sight of God in heaven.[113]

This quote found in Charnock's *The Necessity of Regeneration* does encapsulate the totality, although summative, of what is contained for Charnock in the epistemological strands that have been intertwined in a soul that has been framed in Christ. Contained within this passage is the content of Charnock's works, that is, the attributes of God: "God, as your God and king to protect you, as your Father to cherish you, to the promises, as assurances and deeds for heaven."[114] Once again, Charnock notes the interrelatedness between our conformity to God's holiness and the capacity of knowing him. This is most evident when "the perfectest dress at last of all beautiful grace, which may completely fit you for an everlasting sight of God in heaven."[115] Yet, in each state of knowledge, man still knows according to his capacity, as Peter Martyr Vermigli (1499–1562) notes, "[i]n eternal life the essence of God will be known by the blessed, not of course by the sense but by the soul or mind."[116] This is the case because the "fuller knowledge," asserts Charnock, "is reserved for another life. We must know him here by his name, not by his face; by his grace, not by his glory."[117] This "fuller knowledge" once again draws out the relational aspect of man's conformity and capacity; the saints in heaven "shall know him, as they are known of him,' 1 Cor. 13:12, perfectly, as far as the capacity of a creature can extend."[118] Understandably the creaturely capacity will always be a limiting factor; however, the full measure of that creaturely capacity will be exposed in the heavenly realm and will far excel the most vibrant knowledge in the temporal realm, which is incomprehensibly far short of that in the heavenly realm.[119]

---

113. Charnock, "The Necessity of Regeneration," in *Works*, 3:66–67.
114. Charnock, "The Necessity of Regeneration," in *Works*, 3:67.
115. Charnock, "The Necessity of Regeneration," in *Works*, 3:66–67.
116. Vermigli, *Common Places*, III.17.394.
117. Charnock, "A Discourse of the Knowledge of God," in *Works*, 4:41.
118. Charnock, "The Necessity of Regeneration," in *Works*, 3:52.
119. Charnock, "A Discourse of the Knowledge of God," in *Works*, 4:87. Earlier in this section, Charnock speaks to the congruity of conformity to God's holiness; the necessity of conformity and the capacious epistemological nature of man which is indicative of the intrinsic relation of this conformity and knowledge; "the clearer our knowledge, the closer our adherence." See Charnock, "A Discourse of the Knowledge of God," in *Works*,

VI

The Pneumatological Aspect of Conformity

IN THE OPENING OF his chapter "The Witness of the Spirit in Puritan Thought," from *A Quest for Godliness*, J. I. Packer wrote the following about the ministry of the Holy Spirit in the Puritan theology: "The work of the Holy Spirit is the field in which the Puritans' most valuable contributions to the church's theological heritage were made."[1] This sentiment expressed by Packer appears to be an echoing of B.B. Warfield's assessment of the Reformed doctrine of the Holy Spirit which is noted in the

---

4:60. Therefore, "we must not presume," says Charnock, "to expect an admittance to the vision of God's face, unless our souls be clothed with a robe of holiness, Heb. 12:14." See Charnock, "A Discourse upon the Wisdom of God," in *Works*, 2:66. Flavel would say that there must be an inscription on the spiritual altar that reads: "Holiness to the Lord." See Flavel, *The Whole Works of the Reverend John Flavel*, 3:158. This notion of "imitation" or we could say conformity, is the very thing that John Howe (1630–1675), an English Puritan theologian, identifies as being an epistemological thread which the "glorified souls way of knowing, is an imitation; as the very words seeing and beholding (which it is so frequently set forth by in scripture) do naturally import." Furthermore, "their own holiness," says Howe, "is a conformity to his; the likeness of it" and this has an inherent transforming nature to the capacity of knowing, that is, according to Howe, and "as their beholding it, forms them into that likeness, so that likeness makes them capable of beholding it with pleasure." See Howe, "The Blessedness of the Righteous," in *Works*, 2:65.

1. Packer, *A Quest for Godliness: The Puritan Vision of the Christian Life*, 179. The significance of the Holy Spirit is the epicenter for the Puritan worldview and theological structure, as well as the sum and substance of the spiritual reality found in the new creature. See Embry, "John Flavel's Theology of the Holy Spirit," 84–99. See Nuttall, *The Holy Spirit in Puritan Faith and Experience*. See Beeke and Jones, *A Puritan Theology: Doctrine for Life*, 419–42. See J. K. Parratt, "The Witness of the Holy Spirit: Calvin, the Puritans and St. Paul," 161–68.

introduction of Abraham Kuyper's, *The Work of the Holy Spirit*. Warfield states the following:

> Thomas Goodwin's treatise on "The Work of the Holy Ghost in Our Salvation" is well worthy of a place by its side; and it is only the truth to say that Puritan thought was almost entirely occupied with loving study of the work of the Holy Spirit, and found its highest expression in dogmatico-practical expositions of the several aspects of it—of which such treatises as those of Charnock and Swinnerton on Regeneration are only the best-known examples among a multitude which have fallen out of memory in the lapse of years.[2]

Although Charnock does not have a discourse pertaining to the Holy Spirit, in an of himself, this should not cause one to question whether the Holy Spirit is of importance to Charnock's understanding of the redemptive work. As Warfield noted above, Charnock's works on Regeneration are exemplary works on the Spirit. It could be further suggested that the reason Charnock does not have a specific discourse on the Spirit of God is because of the magnitude of the Spirit's work is implicated in all of God's redemptive work. Hence, we find that the work of the Spirit is the thread that binds the totality of God's redemptive work together in Charnock's thought, and this is evident throughout his discourses. To suggest otherwise would only indicate a lack of exposure to Charnock's works, more specifically, his understanding of the redemptive work of the Spirit in, not only redeeming the soul, but also the framing of the soul to the imitable perfections of God. "Power is a title," declares Charnock,

> belonging to him . . . that great power of changing the heart, and sanctifying a polluted nature, a work greater than creation, is frequently acknowledged in the Scripture to be the peculiar act of the Holy Ghost. The Father, Son, Spirit, are one principle in creation, resurrection, and all the works of omnipotence.[3]

This one principle in creation and resurrection is the work of the Trinity.[4] The totality of man's heart is in the hands of the Trinity, for

---

2 Kuyper, *The Work of the Holy Spirit*, xxviii.

3. Charnock, "A Discourse upon the Power of God," in *Works*, 2:169.

4. Charnock also speaks of the work of the Trinity in the resurrection of Christ and employs similar language, such as, "more glorious than a single creation." Here is his detailed description of the "whole Trinity" in the work of resurrection of Christ. "And this resurrection was more glorious than a single creation, in regard of the mighty load of

Charnock, there is no other way to account for the sustaining nature of a new life that the soul has in Christ. That is, it must be built upon and conformed to the redemptive work of the "whole Trinity." Hence, the reason that Charnock identifies the entirety of the new creature through the redemptive work of the "whole Trinity."

a. The Whole Trinity in the Soul's Conformity

Before further consideration of the "whole Trinity" in Charnock's theological system, it is essential to point out that he employs the "whole Trinity" seven different times in his discourses. He uses it about the goodness of God in the creation of man: it "was a distinct goodness of the whole Trinity," notes Charnock, and "without those raised expressions and marks of joy and triumph as at man's restoration."[5] It is with that usage in mind that we can proceed to consider this "whole Trinity."

It is the "whole Trinity" in the work of reframing the soul to that lost image of God; in the reconciliation, the "whole Trinity is concerned in it" and this is identified in the fact that each "person acts a distinct part."[6] The glory of contriving is appropriated to the Father, as he that made the first motion, counselled Christ to undertake it, sent him in the fulness of time, and bruised him upon the cross, making his soul an offering for sin. The glory of effecting it is ascribed to the second person, both in the satisfactory part to the justice of God, and in the victorious part, the conquest of Satan. The glory of working the conditions upon which it is enjoyed, and the applying it, is attributed wholly to the Spirit.[7]

---

guilt Christ lay by imputation under when upon the cross. It is true this resurrection was the work of the Trinity, it was the work of the Spirit; he is therefore said to be 'quickened by the Spirit,' 1 Pet 3:18, and 'justified in the Spirit,' 1 Tim. 3:16. His resurrection was the justification of his person in all that he performed for the satisfaction of God. Christ also is said to raise himself: John 2:19, 'I will raise it up,' and had an authority to 'take up his life again,' John 10:18. As he is said to conquer his enemies, 1 Cor. 15:25, 'he must reign, till he hath put all enemies under his feet'; yet the Father is said to do it, Ps. 110:1; for acts of power are more peculiarly ascribed to the Father, and resurrection is an act of omnipotence, as wisdom is ascribed to the Son, and love to the Holy Ghost." See Charnock, "A Discourse of God's Being the Author of Reconciliation," in *Works*, 3:436.

5. Charnock, "A Discourse of the Word, the Instrument of Regeneration," in *Works*, 3:319.

6. Charnock, "A Discourse of God's Being the Author of Reconciliation," in *Works*, 3:341.

7. Charnock, "A Discourse of God's Being the Author of Reconciliation," in *Works*,

However, in precluding the creature in this activity does not diminish the personal work of the Trinity in the soul of man, especially in framing the soul to the holiness of God, that imitable perfection. This intimate aspect of redeeming reality is found in the Trinity and Charnock conveys this truth by pointing out that it is the "whole Trinity [which] concern themselves in man's recovery." Not only is the whole of the Trinity involved in this redemptive work, but each is functioning in their necessitated role to bring about the recovery of man's soul. That is, according to Charnock, "the Father contrives it, the Son lays the foundation of it in his blood, the Spirit prepareth the soul for the participation of it."[8] This aspect of scriptural metaphysics (spiritual realm as well–resurrection) is of utmost necessity, and the necessitation of it is identified in the fact that there "is not a fourth person to step in with any operations,"[9] contends Charnock. This very reality establishes the boundary of man's environment, whether it is considered metaphysically, epistemologically, and ethically. As Charnock asserts,

> [t]he whole Trinity, and their personal operations, are particularly offered and slighted, the mercy of the Father, the satisfaction of the Son, and the importunity of the Spirit; since therefore there is no other God, no other Father, no other Son, no other Spirit superior to those, no other world under the government of another God, that any man can transport himself into (as a man may do upon the earth, pass into one country, when he hath offended the laws of another), where is there any relief?[10]

Hence, the new life in Christ brings us into a relational standing with the whole the Trinity. That is, we have "by the new creation, a relation to the blessed Trinity,"[11] and the binding agent of that relation is directly grounded in the Spirit of God, bringing life to a soul.

b. The Centrality of the Spirit in Conformity

In chapter 3 there was the discussion of Charnock's perspective of the *creatio ex nihilio* and the new-creature as "a reality the soul partakes of; it gives a real denomination, a new man, a new heart, a new spirit, a new creature,

3:341.
8. Charnock, "A Discourse of Conviction of Sin," in *Works*, 4:210.
9. Charnock, "A Discourse of the Misery of Unbelievers," in *Works*, 4:317.
10. Charnock, "A Discourse of the Misery of Unbelievers," in *Works*, 4:317.
11. Charnock, "A Discourse of the Nature of Regeneration," in *Works*, 3:137.

something of a real existence; it is called a resurrection."[12] This resurrection is, indeed, the work of the Trinity within the redeemed soul and that work is quickening work, as well as a "washing off our stains [which] is the proper work do the Spirit."[13]

The centrality of the Spirit in Charnock's theological system of thought is made evident in his declaration of this truth in *A Discourse of the Efficient of Regeneration*. In this particular discourse, he identifies the Trinity as the only source of the redemptive work in the soul which precludes the creature from bringing about this redeeming work. It is "to the whole Trinity," propounds Charnock, "without the conjunction of any creature; to the Father as the author, therefore called, 'Our Father' to Christ, as the pattern; to the Spirit, as the inspirer of that grace whereby we are made the sons of God."[14] Charnock goes as far as to equate the reality of grace with the work of the Spirit, "[t]he work of grace is the work of the Spirit,"[15] avers Charnock. That is, this gracious work of the Spirit is a wooing grace to the redeemed soul which is "led by the Spirit, Rom. 8:14, not dragged, not forced; the putting a bias and aptitude in the will, is the work of the Spirit quickening it."[16] It is the grace of the Spirit, the quickening work of the Spirit; however, the reality of the centrality of the Spirit's work is identified in the simple fact that the principle of holiness that infuses life in the soul would not exist apart from the Spirit. "It is called a holy Spirit," explains Charnock, "because without it there can be no holy nature."[17] It is by the effectual application of the work of Christ, that is, the application of the redemption purchased by Christ that the dead man is brought to life by the renewing of the Holy Spirit. This work

---

12. Charnock, *The Doctrine of Regeneration*, 109. The necessity that Charnock speaks of in the realness of this creation cannot be anything other than this "real existence." If it is other than this "real existence" then the whole of his system would collapse or, perhaps, be nothing more than a fanciful construction of the mind that would produce nothing new in a life (other than some meager explorations of man's deceptive imagination about what he cannot even correctly imagine himself capable of). It would be mere imagery without the substance–form without matter.

13. Charnock, "A Discourse of the Cleansing Virtue of Christ's Blood," in *Works*, 3:504.

14. Charnock, "A Discourse of the Nature of Regeneration," in *Works*, 3:252. Charnock notes the following about Rom 8:14, "That place may be reduced to conversion, though the proper meaning is not of conversion."

15. Charnock, "A Discourse of the Nature of Regeneration," in *Works*, 3:245.

16. Charnock, "A Discourse of the Nature of Regeneration," in *Works*, 3:89.

17. Charnock, "The Necessity of Regeneration," in *Works*, 3:79.

Calvin sums up as follows: "the Holy Spirit is the bond by which Christ effectually unites us to himself."[18]

Charnock's understanding of conformity in the new creature in Christ and the stabilizing factor of that new creature's conformity must be in the Spirit of God. If not, there never really was any substantive conformity, rather a mere illusion of conformity. There is a substantive reality of preservation that must accompany the work of the whole Trinity in the soul. To entertain the notion or question of whether or not "we shall persevere if grace doth continue," according to Charnock, is a ridiculous notion which is along the lines of suggesting that "a man shall live to-morrow if his life remain in him, or whether the sun shall shine to-morrow if its light continues; and is as much to say, a man shall persevere if he doth persevere." The question is not if the grace of God will preserve us; instead, insists Charnock, it is "whether the habit of grace, the fear of God, faith, the new creature, new man, or howsoever you will term it, be not so settled in the soul as that it shall never be totally removed."[19] The

---

18. Calvin, *Institutes*, 3.1.1.

19. Charnock, "A Discourse Proving Weak Grace Victorious," in *Works*, 5:254. Due to the limits of this paper, the notion of "habit of grace" is not further developed; however, there is a rich historical discussion associated with the significance of the notion "habit of grace." Charnock makes clear his understanding of the content contained in the habit of grace. In Charnock's, *A Discourse of the Nature of Regeneration*, there is a similar expression when Charnock is addressing the nature of the "habitual grace," which is identified as "the principle of all supernatural acts, as the soul concurs as an immanent principle to all works by this or that faculty." He further points out, "As Christ had a body prepared him to do the work of a mediator, so the soul hath a habit prepared it to do the work of a new creature. To this purpose, there is a habit of truth or sincerity in the will, and a 'hidden wisdom' in the understanding, Ps. 51:6. As the corrupt nature is a habit of sin, so the new nature is a habit of grace; God doth not only call us to believe, love, and obey, but brings in the grace of faith, and love, and obedience, bound up together, and plants it in the soil of the heart, to grow up there unto eternal life; he gives a willingness and readiness to believe, love, and obey." See Charnock, "A Discourse of the Nature of Regeneration," in *Works*, 3:106. I do wonder, with Charnock's words as mentioned above, if we find some of St. Anselm's thought finding its way into Charnock's. It is here that we see, perhaps, the extent of his agreement with Anselm's understanding of faith and its relation to the will. That is, when this new principle is implanted into the soul "God doth not only call us to believe, love, and obey," says Charnock, "but brings in the grace of faith, and love, and obedience, bound up together, and plants it in the soil of the heart, to grow up there unto eternal life;" accordingly Charnock notes, "he gives a willingness and readiness to believe, love, and obey." The following is a similar expression found in Anslem. "It may, therefore, be said, with sufficient fitness," says Anselm, "that living faith believes *in* that *in* which we ought to believe; while dead faith merely believes that which ought to be believed." See Anselm, *Proslogium; Monologium; An Appendix, in Behalf of*

preservation of the new creature that is grounded in the will of God and his grace cannot be uprooted, which suggest that one cannot fall from faith and become enslaved to sin, because the grounding is anchored in the work of the Father, Son, and the Holy Spirit.

There was no room for doubt in the doctrine of regeneration where Charnock placed his anchor (in the Sovereignty of God and His Word), and he had plenty of company in that camp with other Puritans. It is here that he paints a graphic picture of the infinite power of God's Spirit in regeneration, which, Owen summed up as "an inward almighty secret act of the power of the Holy Ghost,"[20] and for Charnock, this is a fundamental and powerful reality. This act may be the re-creative power of the Spirit; however, the impact of this "secret act" quickly becomes evident in manifesting the glorious power contained in the work of the Spirit in conjunction with the Word. This re-generational reality, according to Charnock, will manifest itself because the "heart is ripped open, our putrefied condition in our blood evidenced, our deplorable state unfolded, and thereby the conscience awakened to sensible reflections."[21] Yet, Spirit does not stop at exposing the heart; instead, the Spirit and Word "discovers the secret reserves, unravels the thoughts, pursues sin to its recesses, and pulls and brings it out, as Joshua the king to execution."[22] This is the mighty "secret act" of the Spirit of God when his Spirit is sent forth with his Word. Let that "word be whispered by the Spirit in the ears of a rebel sinner," Charnock declares, "and the curtains which obscured his sin from his eye, drawn open, that he may see what a nest of devils he has, what astonishment will it raise in him."[23] So, Charnock describes the new creature that is brought into existence by the work of regeneration, within the boundaries of the scriptural truths. These scriptural boundaries also identify the substantial consequential nature of the work of the Spirit in the living soul. "Regeneration is," Charnock asserts, "a mighty and powerful change, wrought in the soul by the efficacious working of the Holy Spirit, wherein a vital principle, a new habit, the law of God, and a divine nature,

---

the Fool, by Gaunilon; and Cur Deus Homo, 141.

20. Owen, "Discourse Concerning the Holy Spirit," in *Works*, 3:320.

21 Charnock, "A Discourse of the Word, the Instrument of Regeneration," in *Works*, 3:318.

22. Charnock, *The Doctrine of Regeneration*, 306.

23. Charnock, *The Doctrine of Regeneration*, 306.

are put into, and framed in the heart, enabling it to act holily and pleasingly to God, and to grow up therein to eternal glory."[24]

It is, therefore, the robust operation of the Holy Spirit that infuses the vital principle of holiness into the heart and in the inward framing of the soul to the imitable perfections of God, which requires that the heart is threaded by the grace of the Spirit of God.[25] It is appropriate to reference this work in the heart as being threaded by grace because it is not just one particular faculty that is being redeemed; rather, as Charnock points out, the "Spirit is busy about every part in the formation of the new creature."[26] Moreover, within every part the Spirit is busy shedding the love of Christ into every aspect of the soul, that is, "into every chink and cranny of the soul," posits Goodwin,

> thirsting after this love, and bring[ing] it as fresh as the mother's milk comes out of the dug into the child's mouth or stomach; and his love so shed into us by the Holy Spirit, is digested or turned into love in us, and returned on our parts towards God and Christ again.[27]

This directing of the soul is the centrality of the Spirit's work in fashioning the soul to conform to the image of Christ in knowledge, righteousness, and holiness—that all parts be fashioned to that imitable perfection of God and in fashioning the Spirit instills "a true fire . . . the love of God." Therefore, "he that hath a true sense of God cannot but," says Charnock, "love him, trust in him, humble himself before him, hope in him, resign up himself to him, and bless and press him for his manifestation."[28] Hence, the reason that Calvin concluded that it is "the secret energy of the Spirit, by which we come to enjoy Christ and all his benefits."[29]

---

24. Charnock, "A Discourse of the Nature of Regeneration," in *Works*, 3:87-8. Charnock continues this thought and draws out the consequential reality of this work of regeneration. "Regeneration is by the immediate operation of the Spirit, therefore called 'the sanctification of the Spirit'; the matter of that is without us, the righteousness of Christ; the matter of the other within us, a gracious habit. The form of the one is *imputing*, the form of the other is *infusing* or putting into us; they differ in the end, one is from *condemnation* to *absolution*, the other from *pollution* to *communion*." See Charnock, "A Discourse of the Nature of Regeneration," in *Works*, 3:90.

25. Charnock, "The Necessity of Regeneration," in *Works*, 3:33.

26. Charnock, "A Discourse of the Nature of Regeneration," in *Works*, 3:96.

27. Goodwin, "Of the Work of the Holy Ghost in Our Salvation," in *Works*, 6:25-26.

28. Charnock, "A Discourse of the Knowledge of God," in *Works*, 4:42.

29. Calvin, *Institutes*, III.i.1.

c. The Hemming of Conformity in the Soul

It was mentioned earlier that you get a sense throughout Charnock's writings that if we could get a clear close-up view of the soul's disposition, viewed under a scope, we would find that the reality of grace and holiness forms the constituent parts. For Charnock, grace is the needle, and holiness is the thread that the Spirit weaves throughout the entirety/totality of the soul's complexion. The resultant reality is that there is a continuity in the conformity in a soul framed in Christ.

The conjunctive reality (holiness and grace) is brought to life in the soul by way of Christ's great redemptive work. Whereby the Spirit in its application to the whole of man, it is here that this conjunctive reality is stitched—hemmed in—into the new creaturely reality of grace and holiness, much like, for example, the hemming of a rug. By definition, a hem is a finishing method employed in sewing a garment, in order for the edge of a piece of material—which is folded narrowly and then stitched—to preclude unraveling of the fabric. This idea of a hem gives us an insight into the work of the Spirit of God in the creature who has been newly created in Christ. It speaks to the reality that grace and holiness have been hemmed in the new creature by the Holy Spirit to prevent fraying of that soul that has been framed in Christ. The hem is to maintain the integrity of that shape or design found in the soul's disposition. The whole of the soul's integrity in the framing is grounded in "whole Trinity"—that is, God "is the fountain, the Son is the pattern, and the Holy Ghost the immediate imprinter of this stamp of holiness upon the creature."[30] The "imprinter of this stamp" speaks to the eternal reality infused within the soul; better yet, the eternal reality that the Spirit of God has hemmed within the soul. It is, what Sibbes described as "the gracious frame of holiness set up in our hearts by the Spirit of Christ."[31] If the new creature's reality is anything less than the fabric of grace weaved throughout the soul by hemming work of the Spirit, then the whole nature of the soul's framing is sure to unravel and fall into pieces.

This glorious work of the "whole Trinity" is a degree of reality that we cannot fully grasp; however, in the process of the Trinity working within the framing of the soul to the imitable perfections of God, we become more discerning of the beautiful workmanship within the soul. Charnock depicts

---

30. Charnock, "A Discourse upon the Holiness of God," in *Works*, 2:215.
31. Sibbes, "The Bruised Reed and Smoking Flax," in *Works*, 1:78.

this in terms of having a vision of an object that is far off, as opposed to an object that is up close. In Charnock's words:

> There is a knowledge, before this work of the Spirit, but as of things at a distance. Many know the things proposed in the gospel, but they know it not as a glorious gospel, nor see the wonders in this law, till the Spirit brings that and the faculty close together. As a man may discern a statue or picture at a distance, but till the eye and the objects meet close together, it cannot discern the beautiful workmanship upon them with any affection to them.[32]

This "beautiful workmanship" is the result of the "whole Trinity," and is woven throughout the soul by the Spirit of God. Charnock often refers to this interlacing element of God's Spirit within the soul. For example, in speaking of God's wisdom in his creational design, Charnock contends that

> [i]n this universal conspiring of the creatures together to one end, is the wisdom of the Creator apparent, in tuning so many contraries as the elements are, and preserving them in their order, which, if once broken, the whole frame of nature would crack, and fall in pieces. All are so interwoven and inlaid together by the divine workmanship, as to make up one entire beauty in the whole fabric; as every part in the body of man hath a distinct comeliness, yet there is, besides, the beauty of the whole, that results from the union of diverse parts precisely fashioned to one another, and linked together.[33]

Indeed, Charnock would agree with Calvin, concluding that the Holy Spirit is "the root and seed of heavenly life in us."[34] Therefore, "How great a foundation then is laid in this for your happiness!" declares Charnock, "New creatures, divine nature, a relation to God, the delight of heaven." This relation is a real relationship that we a brought into, built up in, established, and conformed to the imitable perfections of God by his Spirit and it is "upon the account of this relation we know there will be an exact likeness between him and us."[35]

---

32. Charnock, "A Discourse of the Efficient of Regeneration," in *Works*, 3:281–82.
33. Charnock, "A Discourse Upon the Wisdom of God," in *Works*, 2:26.
34. Calvin, *Institutes*, III.i.1.
35. Charnock, "A Discourse of the Nature of Regeneration," in *Works*, 3:138.

VII

Conclusion

This study concludes that Charnock's doctrine of the renewal of the image of God in a soul is a presentation of the dynamic scriptural reality of new spiritual life contained in a soul that has, through the redemptive work of the Trinity, been framed in Christ. Charnock was aware of the depths of reality contained in that part of his question as to what greater excellence can there be than to have a divine beauty impressed upon the soul. For Charnock, this was pointing to a reality that can only be grasped to a certain degree, both here in the temporal, as well as that heavenly realm. Nonetheless, he had a deep hunger to grasp, perceive, understand, and know, to the extent possible, that glorious truth while in this temporal realm. There is, indeed, only one means of being exposed to and glimpsing this divine beauty, and that is through the redemptive work of the whole Trinity. Otherwise, the substance of Charnock's question finds itself in a difficult, if not impossible, situation where the answer is unattainable. Furthermore, the reality contained in his question cannot be real for a soul that stands bent on depravity before the holy Creator; rather, it is caught in a realm of contrarieties incapable of knowing that divine beauty that is covenantally demarcated.

Charnock writes in a summative manner that this conforming reality in the soul and the totality of it is centered upon a harmony that is covenantally circumscribed upon a redeemed soul. In describing this covenantal harmony, Charnock speaks with cause-and-effect relation. That is, the effect of faith is love, and the effect of a renewed soul is a holistic harmony in the soul. This covenantal harmony is demonstrated by Charnock in the following summative statement:

> A supernatural renewing grace must expel corrupt habits from the will, and reduce it to its true object. When faith is planted, it brings love to work by; when the soul is renewed, there is an harmony between God and the heart, between the mind and the word, between the will and the duty; when the appetite and true taste of the soul is restored in regeneration, then spring up strong desires to apply itself to every holy service: 1 Peter 2:2, 3, 'The sincere milk of the word' is fervently desired, after it is spiritually tasted.[1]

What we see is that the covenantal harmony becomes a functional aspect of reality that operates as an ultimate backdrop for the soul's disposition that has been framed in Christ. Charnock concludes:

> He that was the author of harmony in his other creatures, could not be the author of disorder in the chief of his works. Other creatures were his footsteps, but man was his image: Gen. 1:26, 27, 'Let us make man in our image, after our likeness'; which, though it seems to imply no more in that place than an image of his dominion over the creatures, yet the apostle raises it a peg higher, and gives us a larger interpretation of it: Col. 3:10, 'And have put on the new man, which is renewed in knowledge after the image of him that created him'; making it to consist in a resemblance to his righteousness.[2]

The Heavenly Experience in the Temporal

The fundamental question which Charnock to answer was: "Can there be a greater excellency than to have a divine beauty, a formation [connectivity of holiness and grace] of Christ, a proportion of all graces [continuity in conformity], suited [epistemological strands] to the imitable perfections of God?"[3] Although it is rhetorical, it nonetheless operated as a framework to explore the glorious reality of the truth of a soul that is renewed in Christ. In large part, what Charnock identifies in response to this probing question was that the "greater excellency" is when the soul is brought to reflect that imitable perfection of God and redound the Creator's glory.

1. Charnock, "The Necessity of Regeneration," in *Works*, 3:34.
2. Charnock, "A Discourse upon the Holiness of God," in *Works*, 2:205.
3. Charnock, "A Discourse of the Nature of Regeneration," in *Works*, 3:135.

It becomes clear as we have worked through Charnock's theological framework, as it pertains to the renewal of God's image in the soul, that Charnock is not locked into one realm. Instead, he is determined to pull the new reality of heaven into the temporal realm for the soul to taste those heavenly realities. That is, the one realm—temporal—is an opportunity for the new creature to experience the heavenly realm. This is nothing short of Charnock pointing out the degree of impact that the heavenly reality influences the temporal realm, especially within the framing of the soul. This new creaturely reality is "the new creature having the image of God," asserts Charnock, which "hath a model of heaven."[4] And this heavenly model is manifested here in the temporal realm, and the perfection will be had in the heavenly realm. That is, the soul is meant in this temporal realm to partake in heavenly reality,[5] which is depicted in a manner to show that it is not only the beginning of this change but the progress of it till it arrives at perfection.[6] "A drop of grace," says Charnock, "is a drop of glory; so much as there is of the new creation, so much of heaven is put into the soul."[7] What is contained in that portion of heaven that has been placed in the soul? It is what Charnock identifies in the Scripture as "'a lively hope' of heaven here, and a full enjoyment of heaven hereafter, that the soul is 'begotten unto,' 1 Peter 1:3, 4."[8]

Intrinsic within Charnock's understanding of the renewing of the image of God is a progressive aspect of this new creature which is future-oriented, that is, it has an eschatological orientation toward that heavenly realm where the imitable perfections of God will be fully realized. For Charnock, it is genuinely a progressive realization of the most fundamental realities about the nature of the soul that has been renewed in the image of God. Therefore, Charnock concludes that the "greater the progress in this state, the more lively are the hopes of it, and the nearer approaches of heaven to the soul; such a foundation of happiness, with the hopes and foresight of it, cannot but be attended with unconceivable pleasure."[9]

4. Charnock, "A Discourse of the Nature of Regeneration," in *Works* 3:138.

5. Charnock, "The Existence of God," in *Works*, 1:162. The heavenly reality experienced in the temporal realm, "In his soul," says Charnock, "he partakes of heaven, in his body of the earth."

6 Charnock, "A Discourse of the Knowledge of God," in *Works* 4:43.

7 Charnock, "A Discourse of the Nature of Regeneration," in *Works* 3:138.

8 Charnock, "A Discourse of the Nature of Regeneration," in *Works* 3:138.

9. Charnock, "A Discourse of the Nature of Regeneration," in *Works* 3:138. This progress is "wrought by the word," that is, "the first cleansing of the heart, and the progressive

Epistemological Realization of Heavenly Reality

The journey of a soul from a depraved state of existence through the redemptive work of the whole Trinity is a reality that functions in the backdrop of a soul that has been framed in Christ. There is this progressive realization that pertains to the soul that has been renewed in the image of God. Moreover, the progressive realization of this divine beauty is the ongoing work of the Spirit in shaping the image of God and a closer, daily reflection until the perfection of God's imitable perfections is obtained in the heavenly realm.

The most explicit expression of this notion of progressive realization in Charnock's epistemological structure—which is indicative of the relational reality between conformity and the correlative capacity inherent in that conformity—is defined as follows:

> It is a progressive knowledge, still aiming at more knowledge and more improvements of it. Though the knowledge of God be at first infused into us by the inspiration of the Spirit, yet neither that in the head, nor grace in the heart, have their full strength at their first birth, but attain their stature gradually.[10]

This gradual stature of the knowledge of God is directly related to what we as a creature are capable of receiving—knowledge "gives us a sight, and love gives us a possession; we find him by knowledge, but we enjoy him by love." Therefore, concludes Charnock, "Let us improve our knowledge of him for inflaming our affections to him, that we may be prepared for the glory of our eternal life."[11] Hence, the reason that Charnock looks to the capacious epistemological nature as progressive, and for that reason, he emphasizes this progressive nature by noting that

> [w]e go up a mountain step by step, because Christ doth not perform all the parts of his prophetical office at once; there is a further declaration of the name of God to succeed the first: John 17:26, 'I have declared thy name, and will declare it, that the love wherewith thou hast loved me may be in them.' And the ravishments by the virtue and influences of his second shall exceed those of

---

sanctification of it, is wrought by the word: Eph. 5:26, 'That he might sanctify and cleanse it with the washing of water by the word.'" See Charnock, *The Complete Works of Stephen Charnock*, 3:148.

10. Charnock, "A Discourse of the Knowledge of God," in *Works*, 4:60.

11. Charnock, "A Discourse of the Knowledge of God," in *Works*, 4:86–87.

the first revelation, for those further declarations are accompanied with greater manifestations of affection, and fuller communications of divine love to the soul.[12]

It would seem that the substance of the "step by step" is what was in the mind of Charnock as he worked out his theory of knowledge and the reason for the details of that epistemological structure. He distinguishes the various strands and then takes each strand and unravels its content to get a closer view of the fibers that make up that epistemological strand. Take, for example, the experiential strand, which is knowledge pertaining to our experience of scriptural truths. However, this type of knowledge is more complex; it is where Charnock, in his process of extricating the strand, identifies that there are various components to this experiential. What he finds is that within the experiential strand is a higher reality, so to speak, a delightfulness, an intensifying component of our knowledge of God. The intensifying nature of this epistemological strand is expressed when Charnock states that we should "[v]iew God in [our] own experiences of him." Why, or better yet, how does one view God in their experience? The answer to the "why" is found, according to Charnock, in the "taste and sight of his goodness, though no sight of his essence, Ps 34:8. By the taste of his goodness, you may know the reality of the fountain, whence it springs and from whence it flows. This surpasses the most exceptional capacity of a mere natural understanding."[13] The edges of man's existence as it pertains to knowledge is here identified, yet not diminished in the sense of knowing the goodness of God.

Also, this further illustrates Charnock's attempt to grasp ahold of the heavenly realm while in the temporal. There are limitations to man's capacity; however, not many press the boundaries of their capacity, and such an approach—or lack thereof—to our capacity is not acceptable for Charnock. We, indeed, have a great capacity that God has placed within our "mere natural understanding," and at the same time, he has created man in such a dynamic fashion which abounds with complexity and diversity (faculties of the soul: mind, emotions, affections, will). This complexity is to be explored in our pursuit of that thing which will cause the speculative to become foundational, the practical to be expressional of, and the understanding to be satisfied. That is, there becomes a "clear sight of God as the supreme good, the understanding is satisfied, the will filled with love, and all the

---

12. Charnock, "A Discourse of the Knowledge of God," in *Works*, 4:60.
13. Charnock, "The Existence of God," in *Works*, 1:181.

desires of the soul find the centre of their rest."[14] Therefore, the necessity of this experiential strand is for the simple and fundamental fact that this "[e]xperience of the sweetness of the ways of Christianity," Charnock contends, "is a mighty preservative against atheism."[15] Yet, it does more than preserve; it is a binding agent, if you will, that covers and saturates the other strands of knowledge. This binding agent is implicated in the following: "Many a man knows not how to prove honey to be sweet by his reason," Charnock notes, "but by his sense; and if all the reason in the world be brought against it, he will not be reasoned out of what he tastes."[16]

The purpose for Charnock presenting the epistemological strands in the manner that he does, is in order that we might grasp the essence of what can be known here in the temporal, as well as having a sight toward that eternal realm where knowledge will be perfected. "Indeed," declares Charnock, "this knowledge of God is imperfect here because of our present state. But some experience there is here answering to the vision hereafter, as a map of that which the soul is travelling to a sight of."[17]

Progressive Conformity to Holiness

The continuity of conformity to God's holiness has an intrinsic relation to our knowledge, that is, "the clearer our knowledge, the closer our adherence."[18] Therefore, "we must not presume," says Charnock, "to expect an admittance to the vision of God's face, unless our souls be clothed with a robe of holiness, Heb. 12:14."[19] Alternatively, Flavel would say that there should be an inscription on the spiritual altar that reads: "Holiness

---

14. Charnock, "A Discourse of the Knowledge of God," in *Works*, 4:95.
15. Charnock, "The Existence of God," in *Works*, 1:181.
16. Charnock, "The Existence of God," in *Works*, 1:181.
17. Charnock, "A Discourse of the Knowledge of God," in *Works*, 4:20. This notion of a vision of heaven is something that Jonathan Edwards would develop in detail. For example, see Edwards, *Ethical Writings*, "Charity and Its Fruits," in *Works*, 8:125. See also, Edwards, "Heaven is a Progressive State," in *Ethical Writings*, 707. "This progress, however, is taken up into his understanding of the Beatifical vision. Edwards gives three accounts of why there is progress in eternal life with God. These grounds I provisionally call anthropological, metaphysical, and theological." Edwards's notion is set forth in Nichols, *Heaven on Earth: Capturing Jonathan Edwards's Vision of Living in Between*.
18. Charnock, "A Discourse of the Knowledge of God," in *Works*, 4:59.
19. Charnock, "A Discourse upon the Wisdom of God," in *Works*, 2:66.

to the Lord."[20] This notion of "imitation" or we could say conformity, is the very thing that John Howe (1630–1675),[21] an English Puritan theologian, identifies as being an epistemological thread which the "glorified soul's way of knowing, is an imitation; as the very words seeing and beholding (which it is so frequently set forth by in scripture) do naturally import."[22] Furthermore, "[t]heir own holiness," proclaims Howe, "is a conformity to his; the likeness of it," and this has an inherent transforming nature to the capacity of knowing. That is, according to Howe, "as their beholding it, forms them into that likeness, so that likeness makes them capable of beholding it with pleasure."[23]

In the progressive aspect of conformity to God's holiness, we find a correlating progressive aspect to the epistemological realization that is operating with the same eschatological perspective. The removal of the "dimness" that defines the epistemological environment of this temporal realm for the brightness of eternity where we shall know as we are known. It is here we find Charnock standing amid a rich inherited history from solid theologians of the past with this notion of the knowledge to be had in the blessed state of eternity. This distinction of knowledge to be had in the temporal compared the eternal realm is something that occupied the Reformers before the Puritans, and the prospect of it would occupy the Puritans in their effort to grasp and taste what could be tasted of that eternal realm in this temporal realm. This epistemological concept is rooted in the scriptures, more specifically, Paul's declaration in 1 Cor 13:12, "For now we see through a glass, darkly; but then face to face: now I know in part; but then shall I known even as also I am known."

The epistemological concept set forth by the apostle Paul would echo throughout the halls of church history, and those men of a reformed conviction would be entirely captivated by this reality. We see it in the echoing of St. Augustine in the Reformers, such as Peter Martyr Vermigli and Henrich Bullinger (1504–1575). For example, Vermigli in postulating this third knowledge that he describes as that face-to-face knowledge to be had by all those who have been called by God. This idea was nothing

---

20. Flavel, *The Whole Works of the Reverend John Flavel*, 3:158.

21. Howe, whom it was said that "He dwelt with great frequency, and almost superhuman eloquence, upon his favorite theme, the happiness of heaven, and spake as if he were already in the veil." See Howe, *The Works of the Reverend John Howe*, 3:74–77.

22. Howe, "The Blessedness of the Righteous," in *Works*, 2:65.

23. Howe, "The Blessedness of the Righteous," in *Works*, 2:59.

new to Vermigli's theological system; instead, we find this concept being taught in many others from that timeframe. Furthermore, this was a critical element that Bullinger focuses on in his sermon on the *Doctrine of God*, he notes, "beholding of God's face is taken for the most exact and exquisite knowledge of God."[24]

When discussing this state of existence, that blessed state, Vermigli appears to break out in a sad reflection of our state of existence while we still "see in a mirror dimly."[25] He gives the following sad depiction of this dim reality reflected in the mirror:

> Our memory is weak and often fails us ... recent information pushes out old information ... So as regards theoretical matters we have in this world little to be happy about ... In practical affairs we also fall far short since we either act wrongly or wander far from perfection in upright acts. Our virtues are maimed and mutilated ... mental troubles or emotions come into play which drag us hither and thither ... one is troubled by disease ... wounded, cut or burned, goes hungry, or is hard pressed by misfortunes or hardships ... poverty ... These and many other things show clearly enough that we must despair of perfect happiness while we live here.[26]

However, this reality check only serves to encourage and not discourage the knowledge, experience, and the reality of what is to come when we no longer see in a mirror dimly; instead, we will be face to face with our Creator, our God, and our Savior. The primary text for Vermigli in dealing with this *prosopopeia*[27] knowledge is 1 Cor 13:12. However, the Italian

---

24. The *Decades of Henry Bullinger*, dec. IV, sermon 3, "Of God and the Knowledge of God," 145. Bullinger describes this "beholding of God's face is taken for the most exact and exquisite knowledge of God."

25. First Cor 13:12 KJV.

26. Vermigli, *Philosophical Works*, 108–9.

27. In addition, there would appear to be tinges of Augustine's theory of acquaintance in reference to knowledge to be found in Vermigli, especially, in context of the third denomination of knowledge, "prosopopeia." See Vermigli, *Philosophical Works*, 136. McLelland notes that Vermigli in his *De Visionibus*, which is a segment from Vermigli's commentary on Judges 6:22, "distinguishes several pairs of opposites: knowledge through the sense or the understanding; by nature or by revelation (signs); as signs only, or substantial; knowledge in this present life or in the future life. These distinctions may be compared with those of Heinrich; he lists some six kinds of knowledge of God including that by visions and divine mirrors, through the figure *prosopopeia*, another by the contemplation of God's works in creation, and another "which is gathered upon comparisons." Both he and Calvin repeat the traditional image of human weakness when looking towards the divine, as if we were to gaze directly at the sun (§; cf. "Resurrection"

A SOUL FRAMED IN CHRIST

reformer was not breaking new ground with his understanding. Instead, he seems to have relied heavily on Augustine in dealing with this passage; Vermigli comments as follows about Augustine's observations:

> About the nature of God to be seen in heaven, he states: "We shall see face to face." He seems thereby to acknowledge a perception [intuitum] of God by our eyes and face, and in one sense ascribes a face to God himself. Augustine replies that there is also a face of the mind when Paul says that now with face uncovered we behold divine things and not with a veil between, as the Jews required when they talked with Moses.[28]

The aforementioned is a mere snippet because there is a great deal more that Augustine said on this particular text, more specifically, the concept of the mirror, which he refers to as "code." Augustine points out that our perception of our knowledge will not be "through any figure signified in either bodily or spiritual vision, as through a mirror in a code, but face to face (1 Cor 13:12), or as was said about Moses, 'mouth to mouth.'"[29] Here Vermigli describes that blessed state of knowing,

---

§19 above). See also The *Decades of Henry Bullinger*, dec. IV, sermon 3, "Of God and the Knowledge of God," 130 ff. McLelland further notes that "Calvin restricts himself to the *duplex cognitio*, Inst. 1.i.5."

28. Vermigli, *Philosophical Works*, 148. In *Common Places* the wording is slightly different, "But what shall we answer unto the words of Paul, who concerning the beholding the nature of God in our country in heaven, saith; We shall see him face to face, and so seemeth to grant unto our face and eyes the power to see God, and after a sort to devise a face for God himself. Augustine answereth, that there is a face also of the mind, because Paul saith, We now behold heavenly things bare faced, not with a veil or covering; as it come to pass with the Jews, when they spoke unto Moses." See Vermigli, *Common Places*, I:29 b.

29. Augustine, *On Genesis*, in *Works*, I/13, bk 12, § 54–56. "Next, however, just as he has been rapt away from the sense of the body to find himself among these bodily likenesses which are seen in Spirit, so too he may be rapt away from these to be carried up to that region, so to say, of things intellectual or intelligible. There, without any bodily likeness the pure transparent truth is perceived, overcast by no clouds of false opinions ... In order to attain that state of undisturbed rest and that vision of inexpressible truth ... The glory of the Lord is to be seen, not through some significant vision, whether of the bodily kind such as we seen on Mount Sinai, or the spiritual such as Isaiah saw or John in the Apocalypse, not in code but clearly to the extent that the human mind can grasp it, depending on God's grace as he takes it up, so that God may speak mouth to mouth with any whom he has made worthy of such conversation—the mouth of the mind not the body."

the mind is holpen, that by these visible creatures, it may arise to the contemplation of God: as Paule teacheth in the first chapter of the epistle to the Romans. But when we shalbe once in the blessed state, we shall have no more need of the helps of cretures; for we shall then inioie immortalitie . . . as touching the knowledge of God, we shall see him face to face. But (saie they) seeing the corporal eie cannot atteine to the essence of God, (as Augustine[30] verie well teacheth in his booke De Videndo Deo:) therefore, least the eye should be destitute of a fit delectation, unto it shall be offered then a wonderfull adoring of the heavens, and beautie of things now renewed; that it may have, not onelie wherewith to delight and reiose it selfe, but also an occasion to wonder at the power and the infinit wisdom of God.[31]

This is the case because the "fuller knowledge" says Charnock, which "is reserved for another life. We must know him here by his name, not by his face; by his grace, not by his glory."[32] This "fuller knowledge," once again, draws out the relational aspect of man's conformity and capacity, the saints in heaven "'shall know him, as they are known of him,' 1 Cor. 13:12, perfectly, as far as the capacity of a creature can extend."[33] Understandably the creaturely capacity will always be a limiting factor; however, the full measure of that creaturely capacity will be exposed in the heavenly realm and will far excel the most vibrant knowledge in the temporal realm which is incomprehensibly far short of that in the heavenly realm.[34]

The height of this renewal of the image of God that has begun in the temporal realm will have a full manifestation in the heavenly realm where its fullness of felicity, as a creature, will "be completed in an eternal

---

30. Augustine, "The Harmony of the Gospels," in *Saint Augustin: Sermon on the Mount, Harmony of the Gospels, Homilies on the Gospels*, 6:235. Augustine states, "At present it will tarry in the faith of believers, but hereafter it will be possible to contemplate it face to face, when He, our Life, shall appear, and when we shall appear with Him in glory. But if any one supposes that with man, living, as he still does, in this mortal life, it may be possible for a person to dispel and clear off every obscurity induced by corporeal and carnal fancies, and to attain to the serenest light of changeless truth, and to cleave constantly and unswervingly to that with a mind thoroughly estranged from the course of this present life, that man understands neither what he asks, nor who he is that put such a supposition."

31. Vermigli, *Common Places*, III.17.394.

32. Charnock, "A Discourse of the Knowledge of God," in *Works*, 4:41.

33. Charnock, "The Necessity of Regeneration," in *Works*, 3:52.

34. Charnock, "A Discourse of the Knowledge of God," in *Works*, 4:87.

marriage."³⁵ So, that which is "most admired," Charnock says, "at last will be the harmony and consent of things, by the skill of infinite wisdom, in conspiring together for the bringing about those ends God aimed at."³⁶ This end that God has aimed at is that conformity, that covenantal harmony within the framing of the soul where "[g]race hath its print from God, and is conformity to the holiness of God, as appearing in his law. It is the image of God."³⁷ This "print from God" by his grace is nothing short of the "drops of God's perfections, they are so exact an image of him,"³⁸ which results in "an harmony and proportion of all graces in the soul to those perfections of holiness which are in God."³⁹ Therefore, Charnock cannot but conclude that the highest perfection there can be for a creature standing in relation to the Creator is conformity to the Creator. Moreover, there can be no greater excellency for that creature than to have a divine beauty, which is a reflective reality of a soul that has had the divine image of God restored. It is in that restored image that the substance of the imitable perfections of God is etched in the soul; that is, "every line in this new image," says Charnock, has been drawn by the blood of Christ.⁴⁰ So, it is that the continuity in conformity in a soul that finds a formation of Christ in it, where that conformity is defined by "a proportion of all graces, [is] suited to the imitable perfections of God."⁴¹

In closing, the ability for the soul to redound the glory of God requires that renewal of the image of God, not only a renewal but an ongoing upholding of grace to support the soul's capacity to redound the glory of God. "If God be the efficient of regeneration," Charnock reasons, "then there is a necessity of the influence of God in all the progress of grace."⁴² The necessity is directly related to the fact that it "is yet imperfect." "The same hand that planted it must also water and dress it . . . What he is the Creator of, is nursed by his providence; what he is the new Creator of, is fostered by a

---

35 Charnock, "A Discourse of God's Being the Author of Reconciliation," in *Works*, 3:368–9.
  36. Charnock, "A Discourse of the Knowledge of God in Christ," in *Works*, 4:146.
  37. Charnock, "A Discourse Proving Weak Grace Victorious," in *Works*, 5:529.
  38. Charnock, "A Discourse Proving Weak Grace Victorious," in *Works*, 5:529.
  39. Charnock, "A Discourse Proving Weak Grace Victorious," in *Works*, 5:529.
  40. Charnock, "A Discourse of the Nature of Regeneration," in *Works*, 3:188.
  41. Charnock, "A Discourse of the Nature of Regeneration," in *Works*, 3:135.
  42. Charnock, "A Discourse of the Efficient of Regeneration," in *Works*, 3:291–2.

succession of grace."⁴³ This progress, therefore, speaks to another necessity; for Charnock, all must be appropriated to God because

> he is the God that calls us, the God that anoints us, the God that carries us, the God that establisheth us, the God that keeps us, and the God that perfects us. He is the author of grace in its first issue, its fruitful sproutings, its delicious ripenings; it depends upon him in creation, preservation, augmentation, as well as natural things depend upon him in all their progressive motions, from one degree to another, as the author of nature . . . The same power that inspires us with life, inspires us with a perpetual continuation of it.⁴⁴

---

43. Charnock, "A Discourse of the Efficient of Regeneration," in *Works*, 3:291–2.
44. Charnock, "A Discourse of the Efficient of Regeneration," in *Works*, 3:291–2.

VIII

Application

Through Stephen Charnock's account of his experiential knowledge and spiritual reality that permeated his soul, God set before us, yet another example of a man changed by His redemptive work. This paper is a simple "breaking of the surface" of Charnock's detailed account. In Charnock's work there is a turning from the shadowy reality of this temporal world to the eternal reality of the world to come, and the outward manifestation of the inner reality that is of inestimable worth wrapped in the righteousness of Christ.

It was not a vacuous description that Mr. Johnson offers up when speaking at his dear friend's, Stephen Charnock, funeral; rather, it was a man describing the substantive reality of Christ that was manifested in the life of a soul. That is, it was a recognition of a piety that was deeply rooted in the depth of the soul with the lively principle of holiness exhibiting itself in Charnock's thought, word, and deed. How else could Charnock be identified by such a rich image, as provided by Johnson, "the rational house of God, Christ's spiritual building, the temple of the Holy Ghost, framed and made up of orthodox doctrines and good works."[1]

A "rational house of God," clearly speaks of a mind that has been renewed in the righteousness of Christ, that seeks to bring "every thought into captivity to the obedience of Christ."[2] In addition, a man who is operating as this "rational house of God" is a man who has been brought into a proper

---

1. Middleton, "Stephen Charnock, B.D.," *Biographia Evangelica*, 445.
2. Second Cor 10:5.

covenantal standing with his Creator, where sweet and intimate communion unfolds. It would seem that to be described as "the rational house of God" is indicative of our rational faculty being employed to the glory of God. It is to make active effort to refine, discipline, and employ this faculty to know to the extent possible that which God has made known.

What can be said of such a reality? Should it not press us today as we encounter such men as Charnock, more specifically, the truths that Charnock found in the Scriptures? Should not such truths cause us to take a moment of pause, or several moments, to reflect on whether our life is an exhibition of that same principle of holiness in our souls? This comes in the form of a question directed at the soul that has been redeemed in Christ: what soul-reality is being exhibited in your thoughts, words, and deeds? Is it an exhibition of the principle of holiness that has been infused within the soul? Or does your exhibition betray a different reality contained in your soul? Or, in the words of Mr. Johnson, is the reality a projection of a soul that is "Christ's spiritual building," a temple of the Holy Spirit, "framed and made up of orthodox doctrines and good works"?

May it be said of us at our passing, as it was of Stephen Charnock, that we were the lovely image of God in such a manner and awareness that our lives were characteristic of holiness and conformity to the glorious beauty of God. And that our knowledge was not only reflected in our words, but all the more reflected in a piety in this life that glimpses that piety to be had in the life to come. And finally, that our piety conformed to the beauty of holiness, which was consistently moving in the direction of our knowledge rooted in faith here and now replaced with an intuitive, face-to-face, knowledge in glory.

Bibliography

The American Heritage Medical Dictionary. 2007. Houghton Mifflin Company 7 May, 2015.

Ames, William. *Conscience with the Power and Cases Thereof.* 1639. Reprint, Norwood, N.J.: Walte J. Johnson, 1975.

———. *The Marrow of Theology.* Translated by John Dykstra Eusden. Grand Rapids, MI: Baker, 1997.

Anselm, Saint. *Proslogium; Monologium; An Appendix, in Behalf of the Fool, by Gaunilon; and Cur Deus Homo.* Translated by Sidney Norton Deane. Chicago: The Open Court, 1939.

Augustine. *On Genesis: A Refutation of the Manichees, Unfinished Literal Commentary on Genesis, the Literal Meaning of Genesis.* The Works of Saint Augustine, vol. 1/13, edited by John E. Rotelle, translated by Edmund Hill, OP. Hyde Park, New York: New City, 2002.

———. *The Happy Life and Answer to Skeptics and Divine Providence and the Problem of Evil and Soliloquies.* Edited by Ludwig Schopp, translated by Denis J. Kavanagh et al., vol. 5. The Fathers of the Church. New York: CIMA, Inc., 1948.

———. "The Harmony of the Gospels," in *Saint Augustin: Sermon on the Mount, Harmony of the Gospels, Homilies on the Gospels.* Edited by Philip Schaff, translated by S. D. F. Salmond, vol. 6. A Select Library of the Nicene and Post-Nicene Fathers of the Christian Church, First Series. New York: Christian Literature Company, 1888.

Aristotle. "De Anima" in *The Works of Aristotle.* Edited by David Ross, vol. 12. Oxford: The Clarendon, 1952.

———. "Ethica Eudemia" in *The Works of Aristotle.* Edited by W. D. Ross, translated by J. Solomon, vol. 9. Oxford: The Clarendon, 1925.

———. *The Metaphysics.* Translated by John H. McMahon. Amherst, NY. Prometheus, 1991.

Aquinas, Thomas. Commentary on Aristotle's *De Anima.* Translated by Kenelm Foster, O.P., and Silvester Humphries, O.P. Nortre Dame, IN: Dumb Ox, 1951.

Bagshawe, William. *Essays on Union to Christ.* London: Nevil Simmons, 1703.

BIBLIOGRAPHY

Barth, Karl. *Church Dogmatics: The Doctrine of God.* Vol. 4. London; New York: T&T Clark, 2004.

Bates, William. *The Harmony of the Divine Attributes in the Contrivance and Accomplishment of Man's Redemption.* London: J. Darby, 1674; repr. Philadelphia: Presbyterian Board of Publication, n.d, 1985.

———. *The Whole Works of the Rev. William Bates.* Edited by W. Farmer, vol. 3. Reprint, Harrisonburg, VA: Sprinkle Publications, 1990.

Baxter, Richard. *The Practical Works of the Rev. Richard Baxter.* 23 vols. Edited by William Orme. London: James Duncan, 1830.

Beeke, Joel R. and Randall J. Pederson, *Meet the Puritans.* Reformation Heritage, Grand Rapids, MI. 2006.

———. and Mark Jones. *A Puritan Theology: Doctrine for Life.* Grand Rapids, MI. Reformation Heritage, 2012.

Boettner, Loraine. *The Reformed Doctrine of Predestination.* Phillipsburg, NJ: P&R, 1932.

Boston, Thomas. *The Whole Works of Thomas Boston.* 12 vols. Edited by Samuel M'Millan. Aberdeen, Scotland: George and Robert King, 1848.

———. *The Whole Works of Thomas Boston: Human Nature in Its Fourfold State and a View of the Covenant of Grace.* Edited by Samuel M' Millan, vol. 8. Aberdeen, Scotland: George and Robert King, 1850.

———. *The Whole Works of Thomas Boston: Memoirs of the Life, Times, and Writings of the Rev. Thomas Boston.* Edited by Samuel M' Millan, vol. 12. Aberdeen, Scotland: George and Robert King, 1852.

———. *The Whole Works of Thomas Boston: Sermons, Part 2.* Edited by Samuel M'Millan, vol. 4. Aberdeen, Scotland: George and Robert King, 1849.

Brooks, Thomas. *The Works of Thomas Brooks.* 6 vols. Edited by Alexander Balloch Grosart. Edinburgh, Scotland: James Nichol; James Nisbet and Co.; G. Herbert, 1866.

Bullinger, Heinrich. *The Decades of Henry Bullinger.* Edited by Thomas Harding. 1849–1852. Cambridge: Parker Society, 1851.

Burgess, Anthony. *Spiritual Refining A Treatise of Grace and Assurance.* London: A. Miller For Thomas Underhill, 1652; reprint, Ames, Iowa: International Outreach, 1990; reprint, retypeset selections from full work, 2 vols., Ames: International Outreach, 1996–1998.

Burroughs, Jeremiah. *The Saints Treasury.* London: T. C. for John Wright, 1654.

Calvin, John and William Pringle. *Commentaries on the Epistles of Paul to the Galatians and Ephesians.* Bellingham, WA: Logos Bible Software, 2010.

———. *Institutes of the Christian Religion & 2.* Edited by John T. McNeill, translated by Ford Lewis Battles, 2 vols. Louisville, KY: Westminster John Knox, 2011.

———. *Institutes of the Christian Religion.* The Calvin Translation Society, 1845.

Canons of Dort. 1619.

Charnock, Stephen. *The Complete Works of Stephen Charnock.* 5 vols. Edinburgh, Scotland: James Nichol, 1864–1866. Reprint, Edinburgh: Banner of Truth Trust, 1985.

———. *Discourses on Christ Crucified.* London: for the Religious Tract Society, 1830.

———. *Discourses on the Existence and Attributes of God.* 2 vols. 1682. Reprint, Grand Rapids: Baker, 1996.

———. *The Doctrine of Regeneration: Selected from the Writings of Stephen Charnock.* Philadelphia: Presbyterian Board of Publication, 1840.

———. *The Sinfulness and Cure of Thoughts.* Minneapolis, MN. Curiousmith Bookshop, 2018.

Cicero. *On Academic Scepticism*. Translated by Charles Brittain. Indianapolis, IN: Hackett Publisihng Co., Inc., 2006.
Citron, Bernard. *New Birth: A Study of the Evangelical Doctrine of Conversation in the Protestant Fathers*. Edinburgh, Scotland: At The University Press, 1951.
Clark, R. Scott. *Caspar Olevian and the Substance of the Covenant, The Double Benefit of Christ*. Grand Rapids, MI: Reformation Heritage, 2005.
Clarkson, David. *The Works of David Clarkson*. 3 vols. 1864. Reprint, Edinburgh, Scotland: Banner of Truth Trust, 1988.
Coceius, Johannes. *The Doctrine of the Covenant and Testament of God*. Translated by Casey Carmichael, vol. 3, *Classic Reformed Theology*. Grand Rapids, MI: Reformation Heritage, 2016.
Cole, Thomas. *A Discourse of Regeneration*. London: for Thomas Cockerill, 1692.
Dedek, John F. *Experimental Knowledge of Indwelling Trinity: An Historical Study of the Doctrine of St. Thomas*. Mundelein, Illinois: Saint Mary of the Lake Seminary, 1958.
Dickson, David. *The Sum of Saving Knowledge: Or, A Brief Sum of Christian Doctrine*. Edinburgh, Scotland: Johnstone, Hunter, & Co., 1886.
Dolezal, James E. *God without Parts: Divine Simplicity and the Metaphysics of God's Absoluteness*. Eugene: OR. Pickwick Publications, 2011.
Edwards, Jonathan. *Ethical Writings*, "Charity and Its Fruits." Edited by Paul Ramsey and John E. Smith, vol. 8, The Works of Jonathan Edwards. New Haven: Yale University, 1989.
———. "None Are Saved by Their Own Righteousness," in *Jonathan Edwards Sermons*. Edited by Kenneth P. Minkema. New Haven, CT: The Jonathan Edwards Center at Yale University, 1728–1729.
———. *Observations Concerning the Scripture Trinity of the Trinity and Covenant of Redemption*. New York: Charles Scribner's Sons, 1880.
———. *Religious Affections*. Edited by John E. Smith and Harry S. Stout, Revised edition, vol. 2. The Whole Works of Jonathan Edwards. Yale University Press, 2009.
Embry, Adam. "John Flavel's Theology of the Holy Spirit." 14, no. 4 (2010) 84–99.
Erdt, Terrence. *Jonathan Edwards, Art and the Sense of the Heart*. Amherst, MA: University of Massachusetts Press, 1980.
Erskine, Ebenezer. *The Whole Works of the Late Rev. Ebenezer Erskine*. Vol. 1. Edinburgh, Scotland: Ogle & Murray, 1871.
Feenstra, Peter G. *Unspeakable Comfort: A Commentary on the Canons of Dort*. Winnipeg, Canada: Premier, 1997.
Fitzgerald, A. and Cavadini, J., 1999. *Augustine through the ages*. Grand Rapids, Mich.: William B. Eerdmans Publishing Company, 741-747.
Flavel, John. *The Whole Works of the Reverend John Flavel*. 6 vols. London; Edinburgh; Dublin: W. Baynes and Son; Waugh and Innes; M. Keene, 1820.
Geybels, Hans. *Cognitio Dei Experimentalis: A Theological Genealogy of Christian Religious Experience*. Leuven, Paris, Dudley, MA: Leuven University Press, 2007.
Gillespie, Patrick. *The Ark of the Covenant Opened Or the Secret of the Lord's Covenant Unsealed in a Treatise of the Covenant of Grace*. London, 1661, idem, *Ark of the Covenant Opened Or a Treatise upon the Covenant of Redemption*. London, 1677.
Gomarus, Franciscus. *Disputatio theologica de libero arbitrio*. Leiden, 1602.
Goodwin, Thomas. *The Works of Thomas Goodwin*. 12 vols. Edinburgh, Scotland: James Nichol, 1861.

BIBLIOGRAPHY

Grebenitz, Elias. *Tractatus theologicus de regenertione, trinbus disputationibus.* Francofurtum ad Viadrum: Becman, 1671.

Gunton, Colin E. *Act & Being: Towards Theology of the Divine Attributes.* Grand Rapids, MI: William B. Eerdmans, 2002.

The Heidelberg Catechism, in German, Latin and English: With an Historical Introduction: Latin. Tercentenary Edition. New York; Chambersburg, PA: Charles Scribner; M. Kieffer & Co., 1863.

Helm, Paul. "Calvin and the Covenant: Unity and Continuity." *Evangelical Quarterly* 55. 1981, 65–81.

Heywood, Oliver. *The Whole Works of the Rev. Oliver Heywood, B.A.* 5 vols. Idle, UK: Printed by John Vint, 1825.

Hoek, Jan. "God Nearby and God Far Away—Stephen Charnock on Divine Attributes." *In die Skrifig* 48, no. 1. 2014, 7.

Hopkins, Ezekiel. *On Glorifying God in His Attributes,* in *The Works of Ezekiel Hopkins, Successively Bishop of Raphoe and Derry.* Edited by Charles W. Quick, 3 vols. 1874; repr. Morgan, PA.: Soli Deo Gloria Publications, 1995–1998.

Hordern, William. *Experience and Faith: The Significance of Luther for Understanding Today's Experiential Religion.* Eugene, OR: Wipf & Stock Publishers, 2002.

Howe, John. *The Works of the Reverend John Howe.* 3 vols. London: William Tegg and Co., 1848.

Jacombs, Thomas. *Morning Exercise Methodized.* London: E.M, 1660.

Jones, Tudur. "Union with Christ: The Existential Nerve of Puritan Piety." *Tyndale Bulletin* 41/2. 1990, 186–208.

Junius, Franciscus. *A Treatise on True Theology: With the Life of Franciscus Junius.* Translated by David C. Noe. Grand Rapids, MI: Reformation Heritage, 2014.

KJV. Electronic ed. of the 1769 edition of the 1611 Authorized Version. Bellingham WA: Logos Research Systems, Inc., 1995.

Kuyper, Abraham. *The Work of the Holy Spirit.* New York; London: Funk & Wagnalls, 1900.

Lee, Hansang. "Trinitarian Theology and Piety: The Attributes of God in the Thought of Stephen Charnock (1628–1680) and William Perkins (1558–1602)." PhD diss., University of Edinburgh, 2009.

Letham, Robert. *The Westminster Assembly: Readings Its Theology in Historical Context.* Phillipsburg, NJ: P & R, 2009.

Louw, Johannes P. and Eugene Albert Nida. *Greek-English Lexicon of the New Testament: Based on Semantic Domains.* New York: United Bible Societies, 1996.

Maccovius, Johannes. *Disputatio Theologica De Regeneratione.* Franekerae: Heynsius, 1625.

Manton, Thomas. *The Complete Works of Thomas Manton.* 22 vols. London: James Nisbet & Co., 1872.

McGowen, Andrew Thomson Blake. "The Federal Theology of Thomas Boston." PhD diss., University of Aberdeen, 1990.

McGraw, Ryan M. *A Heavenly Directory: Trinitarian Piety, Public Worship and a Reassessment of John Owen's Theology.* KG, Gottingen: Vandenhoeck & Ruprecht, 2014.

Mead, Matthew. *The Almost Christian Discovered.* Halifax: NS: Printed by E. Jacobs, 1788.

Merriam-Webster's Collegiate Dictionary. Springfield, MA: Merriam-Webster, Inc., 2003.

Michelson, Jared. "Reformed and Radically Orthodox? Participatory Metaphysics, Reformed Scholasticism and Radical Orthodoxy's Critique of Modernity." *International Journal of Systematic Theology* 20, no. 1. 2018, 104–28.

Middleton, Erasmus. "Stephen Charnock, B.D.," *Biographia Evangelica; or, An Historical Account of the Most Eminent and Evangelical Authors or Preachers*. Oxford University, 1810.

Miller, Perry. "Jonathan Edwards on the Sense of the Heart." *Harvard Theological Review* 41, no. 2 1948, 99–145.

Muller, Richard A. *Dictionary of Latin and Greek Theological Terms: Drawn Principally from Protestant Scholastic*. 1985. Reprint, Grand Rapids: MI: Baker, 2006.

———. *Post-Reformation Reformed Dogmatics: The Rise and Development of Reformed Orthodoxy, ca. 1520 to ca. 1725*. 4 vols. Grand Rapids: MI: Baker Academic, 2003.

New King James Version. Nashville: Thomas Nelson, 1982.

Nichols, James. *Puritan Sermons*. Vol. 5. Wheaton, IL: Richard Owen Roberts, Publishers, 1981.

Nichols, Stephen J. *Heaven on Earth: Capturing Jonathan Edwards's Vision of Living in Between*. Wheaton, IL: Crossway, 2006.

Nuttall, Geoffrey, F. *The Holy Spirit in Puritan Faith and Experience*. Chicago, IL: University of Chicago Press, 1992.

Owen, John. A *Display of Arminianism*. London: Printed by R. Edwards, 1809.

———. *The Doctrine of the Saints' Perseverance Explained and Confirmed*. London: Printed by Leon Lichfield, 1654.

———. An Exposition of the Epistle to the *Hebrews*. 7 vols. Edited by William H. Goold. Edinburgh: Carlisle, PA: Banner of Truth Trust, 2009.

———. *The Works of John Owen*, 16 vols. Edited by William H. Goold. 1965-1968. Reprint, Edinburgh, Scotland: Banner of Truth Trust, 2000.

Packer, J. I. *A Quest for Godliness: The Puritan Vision of the Christian Life*. Wheaton, IL: Crossway, 1990.

Parratt, J. K. "The Witness of the Holy Spirit: Calvin, the Puritans and St. Paul." *Evangelical Quarterly* 41, 1969, 161–68.

Perkins, William. *A Declaration of the True Manner of Knowing Christ Crucified*. Printed by John Legat, Printer, Cambridge, 1600.

———. *The Estate of a Christian in this Life*. London, John Legatte, 1635.

Plato, *Timaeus. Critias, Cleitophon, Menexenus, Epistles: English Text*. Edited by G. P. Goold, translated by R. G. Bury, The Loeb Classical Library. Cambridge, MA; London, England: Harvard University Press, 1929.

Preston, John. *The New Covenant or The Saints Portion*. London: I.D, 1621.

Reuter, Karl. "William Ames: The Leading Theologian in the Awakening of Reformed Pietism," in *William Ames*. Translated by Douglas Horton. Cambridge, MA: Harvard Divinity School Library, 1965.

Reynolds, Edward. *Animalis Homo. Londini; Excudebat T. Newcomb pro R. Bostock, 1650*.

Robertson, O. Palmer. *The Christ of the Covenants*. Phillipsburg, NJ: Presbyterian and Reformed, 1980.

Rollock, Robert. *Selected Works of Robert Rollock*. 2 vols. Grand Rapids, MI: Reformation Heritage, 2008.

Rutherford, Samuel. *Covenant of Life Opened: Or, A Treatise of the Covenant of Grace*. Edinburgh, A.A. for Robert Broun, 1655.

The Savoy Declaration of Faith and Order. 1658. Reprint, London: Evangelical, 1971.

Sibbes, Richard. *The Complete Works of Richard Sibbes*. 7 vols. Edited by Alexander Balloch Grosart. Edinburgh, Scotland: James Nichol; James Nisbet and Co.; W. Robertson, 1863.

Siekawitch, Larry. *Balancing Head and Heart in Seventeenth Century Puritanism, Stephen Charnock's Doctrine of the Knowledge of God*. Milton Keynes, UK: Paternoster, 2012.

Smith, John. *Select Discourses*. London: Cambridge, printed by F. Flesher, 1673.

Smith, John E. "Editor's Introduction," in *Religious Affections*. Edited by John E. Smith and Harry S. Stout, Revised edition., vol. 2, The Works of Jonathan Edwards. New Haven, CT: Yale University Press, 2009.

Stein, Stephen J. "The Quest for the Spiritual Sense: The Biblical Hermeneutics of Jonathan Edwards." *Harvard Theological Review* 70, no. 1/2. April 1977, 99–113.

Strimesius, Samuel. *Tractatus theologicus de regeneratione, tribus disputationibus*. Francofurtum ad Viadrum: Becman, 1671.

Swinnock, George. *The Works of George Swinnock, M.A.* 5 vols. Edinburgh; London; Dublin: James Nichol; James Nisbet and Co.; G. Herbert, 1868.

Toon, Peter. *Born Again*. Grand Rapids: MI Baker Book House, 1987.

Torrance, T. F. *The School of Faith: The Catechisms of the Reformed Church*. London: James Clarke, 1959.

Traill, Robert. *The Works of Robert Traill*. Vol. 1. The Banner of Truth Trust, 1810.

Trueman, Carl R. *John Owen Reformed Catholic, Renaissance Man*. Burlington, VT: Ashgate, 2007.

Turretin, Francis. *Institutes of Elenctic Theology*. Edited by James T. Dennison Jr., translated by George Musgrave Giger, vol. 1. Phillipsburg, NJ: P&R, 1992–1997.

Van Asselt, Willem J, J. Martin Bac, and Roelf T. te Velde. *Reformed Thought of Freedom: The Concept of Free Choice in Early Modern Reformed Theology*. Grand Rapids, MI. Baker Academic, 2010.

Vanderkemp, John. *The Christian Entirely the Property of Christ, in Life and Death: Exhibited in Fifty-Three Sermons on the Heidelberg Catechism*. New-Brunswick, N.J.: Abraham Blauvelt, 1810, vol. 1.

Van Den Berg, J. *The Synod of Dort in the Balance*. Nederlands archief voor kerkgeschiedenis. Dutch Review of Church History, vol. 69, No. 2. 1989.

Van Mastricht, Peter. *Theoretical and Practical Theology Volume 1: Intellectual Prerequisites*. Edited by Joel R. Beeke, translated by Todd M. Rester, vol. 1. Grand Rapids, MI: Reformation Heritage, 2018.

———. *Theoretical and Practical Theology Volume 2: Faith in the Triune God*. Edited by Joel R. Beeke and Michael T. Spangler, translated by Todd M. Rester, vol. 2. Grand Rapids, MI: Reformation Heritage, 2019.

———. *A Treatise on Regeneration*. New-Haven: Printed for Thomas and Samuel Green, 1769.

Van Til, Cornelius and Eric H. Sigward. *Unpublished Manuscripts of Cornelius Van Til*. Electronic ed. Labels Army Company: NY, 1997.

Van Vliet, Jan. *Studies in Christian History and Thought, The Rise of Reformed System, The Intellectual Heritage of William Ames*. Eugene, OR: Wipf & Stock, 2013.

Venema, Cornelius P. *But for the Grace of God*. 2nd ed. Grandville, MI. Reformed Fellowship, Inc., 2011.

Vermigli, Peter Martyr. *Common Places of Peter Martyr Vermigli*. "Translated and partly gathered" by Anthony Marten. London, 1583.

---. *Philosophical Works, On the Relation of Philosophy to Theology.* Edited by Joseph C. McLelland. Kirksville, MO. Truman State University, 1996.

Vos, Geerhardus. *Reformed Dogmatics.* Edited by Richard B. Gaffin, translated by Annemie Godbehere et al., vol. 2. Bellingham, WA: Lexham, 2012–2014.

Walton, Brad. "'Formerly Approved and Applauded' The Continuity of Edwards's Treatise Concerning Religious Affections with Seventeenth-Century Puritan Analyses of True Piety, Spiritual Sensation and Heart-Religion." PhD diss., Wycliffe College, 1999.

Watson, Thomas. "Discourses upon Christ's Sermon on the Mount," in *Discourses on Important and Interesting Subjects, Being the Select Works of the Rev. Thomas Watson.* Vol. 2. Edinburgh; Glasgow: Blackie, Fullarton, & Co.; A. Fullarton & Co., 1829.

---. *The Select Works of the Rev. Thomas Watson, Comprising His Celebrated Body of Divinity, in a Series of Lectures on the Shorter Catechism, and Various Sermons and Treatises.* New York: Robert Carter & Brothers, 1855.

---. *Spiritual Life Delineated; With the Detection and Exposure of Some of the Popular Errors of the Day.* London: R. B. Seeley and W. Burnside, 1838.

Westminster Assembly. *The Westminster Confession of Faith: Edinburgh Edition.* Philadelphia: William S. Young, 1851.

Whatley, William. *The New Birth: Or, a Treatise of Regeneration.* London: Assignes of Thomas Man, 1630.

Willard, Samuel. *A Compleat Body of Divinity in Two Hundred and Fifty Expository Lectures on the Assembly's Shorter Catechism.* Boston, New England: G. Green, S. Kneeland, 1726.

Witsius, Herman. *The Economy of the Covenants between God and Man.* Reprinted Kingsburg, CA: den Dulk Christian Foundation, 1990.

Wright, Scott R. "Regeneration and Redemptive History." Westminster Theological Seminary: PhD diss., 1999.

www.ingramcontent.com/pod-product-compliance
Lightning Source LLC
Chambersburg PA
CBHW072149160426
43197CB00012B/2305